Victory Mission

Messages of Power & Hope

ASHLEY ENNIS

All rights reserved solely by the author. The author guarantees that all contents are original and does not infringe upon the legal rights of any other person or work. No parts of this publication may be reproduced without prior consent of the author.

Scripture taken from the King James Bible.

Scripture taken from The Message. Copyright Â© 1993, 1994, 1995, 1996, 2000, 2001, 2002. Used by permission of NavPress Publishing Group.

Definitions taken from *Vine's Complete Expository Dictionary of Old and New Testament Words* by W.E. Vine. Copyright © 1996 by Thomas Nelson. Used by permission of Thomas Nelson. www.thomasnelson.com

Copyright ©2021 Ashley Ennis

ISBN: 9798477252381

To Jennifer Jones, Terrie Meek, and all my friends at Victory Mission Bible Training Center.

To Laura Meek for introducing me to Victory and for all the laughter she carries with her.

"But thanks be to God, which giveth us the victory through our Lord Jesus Christ." ~1 Corinthians 15:57

CONTENTS

A PLACE FOR VICTORY	1
CROWNED	3
HIDDEN IN CHRIST	10
BILLOWS	15
BLESSED	21
THE DAY OF VISITATION	28
SOLDIER WORDS	34
ANATOMY OF THE HEART	40
AN APPOINTED TIME	51
BRINGING IN THE SHEAVES	56
UNDER NEW MANAGEMENT	63
CHILDREN OF THE PROMISE	69
COME UP HIGHER	77
ESTABLISHED	83
EVERY PRECIOUS THING	89
GLORY, HONOUR & POWER	90
HEALING	105
ISNT HE WONDERFUL?	110
THE JOY OF SACRIFICE	114
EVERY PLACE	118
STAR CHASERS	124
THE PRAYER WHEEL	130
THE FATHER OF LIGHTS	136
THE END OF A THING	143
CONCLUSION	150

For even hereunto were ye called: because Christ also suffered for us, leaving us an example, that ye should follow his steps: Who did no sin, neither was guile found in his mouth: Who, when he was reviled, reviled not again; when he suffered, he threatened not; but committed himself to him that judgeth righteously: Who his own self bare our sins in his own body on the tree, that we, being dead to sins, should live unto righteousness: by whose stripes ye were healed. For ye were as sheep going astray; but are now returned unto the Shepherd and Bishop of your souls.

- 1 Peter 2:21-25

A PLACE FOR VICTORY

The messages in this book come from a year of preaching at Victory Mission Bible Training Center in Center Ridge, Arkansas. Victory is aptly named because it does just that, offers a place for victory. A place to fight the battles of addiction and life controlling behaviors. A place to seek the Lord and find Him. A place to change the outcome for future generations. It is a home, a church, and a refuge for the hurting and the lost.

Describing what happens at Victory would be impossible without the context of the Word of God. Day in and day out, staff and volunteers pour the Word into the hungry hearts of residents, knowing it is only through the work of the Spirit that people are truly changed. It isn't the schedule, the rules, or the expectations that brings the breakthrough, it is the freedom found through repentance and deliverance in the powerful name of Jesus.

People come to Victory for all different reasons and from all different backgrounds. Their testimonies range the breadth of the human experience, and yet there is a common thread of hope that guides them through the process of redemption. The hope that Jesus is still in the business of restoration and that it is never too late to start over. I have personally seen the changes that come through the resident's wrestle with God and their refusal to stop until their blessings come. I have witnessed radical transformations that are nothing short of a miracle and I give God glory for what He is doing through the men and women at Victory that have lived the breakthrough themselves and are now heaping the love of God on the broken vessels they find waiting on their doorstep.

The Builder has set up shop and is changing lives of people from all over the country in the middle of Arkansas, on a small but beautiful campus surrounded by the greenest fields you will ever see. This place of hope is where souls are brought back to life and taught how to "take root downwards and bear fruit upwards" (Isaiah 37:31).

What you will find in the pages ahead are words of encouragement that speak to the heart and build confidence from the ground up. Much of it is scripture and all of it points to Jesus, who is the only way to a radical life of freedom.

It doesn't take much to change, but it takes all you have- a complete surrendering to the will of God for your life. Do you need a different outcome? Are you tired of the hurts and the habits that repeat themselves over and over again, the same actions leading to the same results? Are you looking for Jesus? If so, give Victory a chance.

Victory Mission Bible Training Center
Jennifer Jones, Program Director
750 Austin Road
Center Ridge, Arkansas 72027
Phone: 501.386.1493
www.missionteens.com

CROWNED

"O Lord, our Lord, how excellent is thy name in all the earth! who hast set thy glory above the heavens. Out of the mouth of babes and sucklings hast thou ordained strength because of thine enemies, that thou mightest still the enemy and the avenger. When I consider thy heavens, the work of thy fingers, the moon and the stars, which thou hast ordained; What is man, that thou art mindful of him? and the son of man, that thou visitest him? For thou hast made him a little lower than the angels, and hast crowned him with glory and honour. Thou madest him to have dominion over the works of thy hands; thou hast put all things under his feet: All sheep and oxen, yea, and the beasts of the field; The fowl of the air, and the fish of the sea, and whatsoever passeth through the paths of the seas. O Lord our Lord, how excellent is thy name in all the earth!"

-Psalm 8:1-9

There is a specific type of glory and honour that comes from following Jesus. Psalm 8:5 tells us God Himself placed glory and honour on us as part of our creation, "For thou hast made him a little lower than the angels, and hast crowned him with glory and honour." We can think of the action of being crowned as the victor's crown, a symbol of triumph.

When we choose to follow Jesus, we wear a dignity that cannot be seen through outward appearance. It is a quiet dignity. A humble dignity. A bold dignity. We are counted worthy because He is worthy, and we wear the dignity of His cross.

We are used to giving Jesus glory and honour, but in Psalms 8:5 we see that He also gives us glory and honour. This is how humble Jesus is. He reflects His qualities onto our life.

Did you ever take a mirror and point it at the sun to see the rays bounce off? Our life in Christ is a little like that- when we stand in the power of His Name, the name of Jesus, His qualities and the honor that is due to Him bounces off onto us. His nature is reflected onto our nature. We become like Him, but not completely like Him. We cannot redeem anyone, we cannot get anyone into heaven or restore their soul, but Matthew 10:25 tells us, "It is enough for the disciple that he be as his master, and the servant as his lord."

Amazing…the God of honour and glory has crowned us with honour and glory. He has placed them upon us because we are His:

> But now thus saith the Lord that created thee, O Jacob, and he that formed thee, O Israel, Fear not: for I have redeemed thee, I have called thee by thy name; thou art mine.
> - Isaiah 43:1

Jesus has called you by name. Purposely, with intention, you are His.

There are a lot of people, maybe even most people, who are bad at names. I am one of them. You don't intentionally forget a person's name, it's just that if you are not around them much, or your brain is full of facts and deadlines, the name doesn't seem to be as important as the person, but we know this isn't true. Jesus, Himself, has the name that is above all names. When you get to heaven, He will give you a new name that nobody else knows. He is going to write it on a white stone and hand it to you (Revelation 2:17). I believe it will be one word that sums up His heart for you, a word that will make everything that happened on earth make sense.

Your name means something to Jesus, just as His name means something to you. He thought of you while He bore His stripes, carried His cross, and hung on a tree. To Him, your name means redemption, peace, power, love, salvation, a hope and a future (Jeremiah 29:11).

If your name is written in the Lamb's Book of Life, He has crowned you accordingly. Do you believe what I am saying? Because you are His, He has placed on you the honour and the glory that you will receive in eternity. It is as if you are a prince or a princess next in line to be King or Queen, because He "calleth those things which be not as though they were" (Romans 4:17).

> "And in Him, having heard and believed the word of truth—the gospel of your salvation—you were sealed with the promised Holy Spirit, who is the pledge of our inheritance until the redemption of those who are God's possession, to the praise of His glory" (Ephesians 1:13-14).

You are glorified by God's good opinion of you. Jesus has a good opinion of you, not only that but He delights in you. There is a popular saying, "Opinions are like noses, everybody has one." Every person on the planet has an opinion about something. When we form an opinion, we are sharing the value we think it has. The thing about opinions, however, is they can be based on nothing. I can have an opinion that strawberries are the worst food in the whole world. You can have an opinion that they are the best. Who is right? Both of us? Neither of us? Does it even matter? Our opinion on things holds very little weight in the kingdom of God. What someone thinks about you doesn't matter.

Not caring about a bad opinion is much easier to say than to do. We care about how people see us and if they like us. We care if they think we have value or not. It hurts our souls when we feel rejected, but we must remember that Jesus was also rejected. His rejection was the path to understanding us better. Perhaps your rejection has done the same for you? Who do you pray for and care about for no other reason than you understand how they feel?

Jesus was rejected for you, but Jesus will never reject you.

King David at one time was just the kid that nobody wanted to deal with. When Samuel came to anoint the next king, all of David's brothers came in, but Samuel asked if there was another. David's father hadn't even thought to call him out of the field (1 Samuel 16:11-13).

Later, when Goliath was giving Israel trouble, David was sent to deliver food to the army:
> And David spake to the men that stood by him, saying, What shall be done to the man

> that killeth this Philistine, and taketh away the reproach from Israel? for who is this uncircumcised Philistine, that he should defy the armies of the living God? And the people answered him after this manner, saying, So shall it be done to the man that killeth him. And Eliab his eldest brother heard when he spake unto the men; and Eliab's anger was kindled against David, and he said, Why camest thou down hither? and with whom hast thou left those few sheep in the wilderness? I know thy pride, and the naughtiness of thine heart; for thou art come down that thou mightest see the battle. And David said, What have I now done? Is there not a cause?
>
> -1 Samuel 17:26-29

David's brother, Eliab, didn't have a very high opinion of David, but that didn't make David less anointed. It didn't make David less called. It was simply his brother's opinion. Eliab wanted to send David back down to the sheep, but David was called to do something nobody else wanted to do. David was called to defeat the Philistines.

We live in a world with a lot of opinions and point of views. Everybody has one and they give them out freely and without being asked. For you, child of God, the one who is crowned with glory and honour, the only opinions that matter are the Lord's.

Jesus thinks you are the greatest thing ever. He thinks you are adorable. He delights in your life and your accomplishments. Your efforts and the way you love others makes Him proud.

I have a new puppy named Winston. Winston is a mess. He chases the cat, digs stuff out of the trash, and drags dirty laundry all over the house. Do you know what happens when he does this? I get aggravated for about one minute, then I tell him how cute he is, pick him up and love on him. I think he is adorable, not because of what he does but because he is mine and I love him. I think Jesus sees us a little bit like this. We do things we aren't supposed to do, we repent, turn from it, and Jesus says, "She's the best. She's the greatest. There is nobody as wonderful as her. Do you see how proud I am of her?"

Jesus has a high opinion of you because you keep choosing Him and He loves it. He has crowned you with glory and honour. He has placed you a little lower than the angels and a lot higher than the animals. If I can love Winston enough to forgive him every time he chews the furniture, how much more can the One who made you easily forgive your transgressions? Jesus is slow to anger and quick to forgive (Psalm 103:8).

It bothers us when we think people don't value us or love us, but what matters most is that Jesus has crowned you and called you His, anything other than that truth is under your foot:

> When I consider thy heavens, the work of thy fingers, the moon and the stars, which thou

hast ordained; What is man, that thou art mindful of him? and the son of man, that thou visitest him? For thou hast made him a little lower than the angels, and hast crowned him with glory and honour. Thou madest him to have dominion over the works of thy hands; thou hast put all things under his feet:
                                              -Psalm 8:3-6

HIDDEN IN CHRIST

"Thou art my hiding place; thou shalt preserve me from trouble; thou shalt compass me about with songs of deliverance. Selah."

- Psalm 32:7

There are many verses in Psalms that speaks of God being our hiding place, but I knew this verse was the verse for us when I read the word *compass*.

Compass has several definitions, but the definition that suits this verse and our purposes is one that means to enclose and stretch around. To compass is to take a hold of something and pull it in.

If you can imagine the word compass in your mind's eye, you might imagine a hug. Jesus is a hugger. But it isn't just a little hug, it is the type of hug that pulls you in. Believe it or not there is such a thing as an anointed hug.

The Bible uses the term "fell on his neck" to describe this type of hug. Take, for example, the return of the prodigal son. The prodigal son is our prime example of deliverance. A man who asks for his wealth too early, squanders it on himself, then finding himself with the pigs decides to return to his father in hopes of eating with the servants:

> And when he came to himself, he said, How many hired servants of my father's have bread enough and to spare, and I perish with hunger! I will arise and go to my father, and

> will say unto him, Father, I have sinned against heaven, and before thee, And am no more worthy to be called thy son: make me as one of thy hired servants. And he arose, and came to his father. But when he was yet a great way off, his father saw him, and had compassion, and ran, and fell on his neck, and kissed him. And the son said unto him, Father, I have sinned against heaven, and in thy sight, and am no more worthy to be called thy son. But the father said to his servants, Bring forth the best robe, and put it on him; and put a ring on his hand, and shoes on his feet: And bring hither the fatted calf, and kill it; and let us eat, and be merry: For this my son was dead, and is alive again; he was lost, and is found. And they began to be merry.
>
> -Luke 15:17-24

Notice the father was moved with compassion. Compass is a root word of compassion. The hug was the evidence of his father's compassion. It was the evidence that everything was going to be okay, that all was forgiven, and would soon be made right again. Compassion softens hearts and changes lives. When Jesus moves with compassion the dead are raised, the sick are healed, and the hungry are fed.

Jesus is full of lovingkindness and tender mercies. When He looks at you, He isn't angry. True, God is angry with the wicked every day, but for those with a tender heart to receive Him and know Him, our God's instinct is to draw us in.

When He sees you running towards Him like the prodigal son, He flings open the doors of heaven and runs towards you, encircling you, compassing you with songs of deliverance.

Jesus delivers us from our pain, from our past, from the hand of the enemy, and from the price of sin, but first He had to be delivered into Pilate's Hall.

Jesus could have died easily. He could have taken the quick route or the pain-free path. He could have simply gone straight to the cross, done what He had to do and get it over with, but He didn't. He allowed himself to be beaten so we could gain access to the blood of redemption.

Blood is enclosed in the body. For it to be spilled Jesus had to bare as many stripes as possible. He allowed himself to be beaten to the edge of death. Then, a big, heavy cross was placed on His back, the back that was torn and bleeding, so that the blood of His sacrifice would cover the cross that He would hang on. As if that wasn't enough, He carried that heavy cross up a hill. This wasn't any old cross; it was *HIS* cross, made just for Him. The weight of sin bearing down on His wounds. He didn't have to do it, but He did. And now, we are invited to sit under the cross. He asks us to take shelter under it and be covered in His blood. It's not a sprinkle, it is a covering. It protects us from sin, from wounds, from deep pain. When we plead the blood of Jesus, we receive the benefits of being a follower of Jesus.

He is our hiding place. We are hidden in the blood of Jesus, the One who died so we could live:

> It's obvious, of course, that he didn't go to all this trouble for angels. It was for people like us, children of Abraham. That's why he had to enter into every detail of human life. Then, when he came before God as high priest to get rid of the people's sins, he would have already experienced it all himself- all the pain, all the testing- and would be able to help where help was needed.
>
> -Hebrews 2:16-18 (The Message)

Jesus understands what you are going through, because He has been through it Himself. It may not be the exact situation, but the root of the situation is something He experienced in the years He was on Earth, from birth to His resurrection.

Jesus understands you.

There is nothing you can hide from Him. Nothing He will be shocked by or surprised about. He knows you better than you know yourself and when He sees you, He moves with compassion. He hugs your neck and sings songs of deliverance over you.

Hide in Jesus.
Get lost in His Word.
Find yourself in His story.

Say prayers asking Jesus to have compassion on you and to move in your life in a way that is full of lovingkindness. To preserve you in times of trouble:

"Lord, I pray for compassion.
I pray for mercy.
Do you see me running towards You, Jesus?
I'm giving it all I've got.
I'm using everything that is in me to get closer to You.
Sing to me, Lord, I'm listening.
Hide me, Jesus, I'm Yours."

Nobody will ever love you like Jesus.

So, here is our question: Is there something you need to run to Jesus about? Is there pain you haven't dealt with? Bitterness you won't let rise to the surface? Sin you need forgiveness for? Is there something you need to bring before the Lord because you need it to be dealt with in a way that is loving and gentle?

Jesus won't snatch it from you. He won't be rough with you. He will hug your neck, look you in the eye, and say, "we can deal with this together. You don't have to do it alone."

Shame is from the enemy.
Condemnation is from the enemy.
Guilt is from the enemy.

God is love. Let Him love you.

BILLOWS

"Deep calleth unto deep at the noise of thy waterspouts: all thy waves and thy billows are gone over me."

- Psalms 42:7

"Then Jonah prayed unto the Lord his God out of the fish's belly, And said, I cried by reason of mine affliction unto the Lord, and he heard me; out of the belly of hell cried I, and thou heardest my voice. For thou hadst cast me into the deep, in the midst of the seas; and the floods compassed me about: all thy billows and thy waves passed over me."

-Jonah 2:1-3

The book of Jonah tells us that he was a prophet who was asked by the Lord to go to Nineveh to cry out because of their sin. The problem was that Jonah didn't want to go to Nineveh, so he tried to outrun God. He went the other direction towards Tarshish.

God gave Jonah an assignment and he fled. God put a calling on his life and because he was afraid of the outcome, he went another way. Jonah ran from the presence of God, because in His presence there is nowhere to hide.

Jonah found himself in the belly of a fish, in the bowels of hell. Have you ever been there? In the bowels of hell? What caused it? Most likely it was your own sin. Jonah sinned against God. He was rebellious. He chose his own way, but God pursued him. This isn't the kind of pursuing we like to think about. We like the moments where God chases us down with overwhelming love, but what about the times He chases us straight into the darkness of our own doing? Into the whale of repentance?

In just a few short sentences, Jonah would speak of the whale vomiting him out. Vomiting is a symbol for repentance-getting it all out in a way that is as gut wrenching as it must have been for Jesus to watch happen in the first place, "Behold, O Lord; for I am in distress: my bowels are troubled; mine heart is turned within me; for I have grievously rebelled" (Lamentation 1:20).

Repentance is done from the belly as much as from the heart and the mouth. The prophet Isaiah experienced the epitome of repentance. A repentance that leads to intercession. An intercession that leads to an assignment:

> Then said I, Woe is me! for I am undone; because I am a man of unclean lips, and I dwell in the midst of a people of unclean lips: for mine eyes have seen the King, the Lord of hosts.
> -Isaiah 6:5

Here, we see Isaiah acknowledging his sin. He says, "I am unclean." He then goes on to call out a people beyond himself, "I dwell in the midst of a people of unclean lips." He recognized the unholiness in himself and then called out the unholiness of the people who lived where he lived, realizing they must all be alike. He thought, "I am as my people are. My nature is sin; therefore, your nature is sin." He didn't just repent for himself, he repented as a representative of his people. Do you see what I am saying? You and I can stand in for those who are just like us. We can take on another's sin in repentance. When we do this, we raise our prayer profile. We are promoted in the kingdom. Let us be conformed in this way to the image of Jesus, "For he hath made him to be sin for us, who knew no sin; that we might be made the righteousness of God in him" (2 Corinthians 5:21).

To intercede means to intervene, to reconcile. Jesus intercedes for us. The Spirit intercedes for us in groanings which we ourselves cannot utter (Romans 8:26). God responds to our groaning.

Groaning in repentance does not sound like that much fun. Groaning from your bowels sounds like even less fun, but I am here to tell you there is a place in prayer where you cannot get yourself up off the floor for the weight of the groaning. This is prayer that is often done in secret when it is just you and Jesus. In my experience, this is why the Word commands:
> But thou, when thou prayest, enter into thy closet, and when thou hast shut thy door, pray to thy Father which is in secret; and thy Father which seeth in secret shall reward thee openly.
>
> -Matthew 6:6

We need a place where we can shut the door and be by ourselves and do all the things we have to do to manage what the Lord has put in us. We need the opportunity to commune with the Lord. Repent of our sins. Release burdens. Renew our minds. Refresh our spirits.

The Spirit will draw you into such a deep place of intercession that your earthly body made of flesh is no longer in control because you have lost yourself. The weight of sin nature pulls your belly into the floor, and you will know the end of yourself, that you are a worm and not worthy to be in need of deliverance (Psalm 22:6). This type of prayer will cause you to say, "Woe is me, for I am undone." Then, when you are done repenting over yourself, you will flood your face with tears in intercession because of the sin of the world.

Maybe that sounds dramatic and if I hadn't experienced it, I might agree. I had no idea it was coming. I went into my prayer closet on a Saturday morning trying to understand all the mess that was in the world but when I left my closet, I was a different person. I had been through something with the Lord. He and I came to an understanding about who He was and who I was. Not in a way that was unloving, but in a way that was true. He is holy and I am not. He is all-knowing and I am not. He is God and I am not. It is by His grace that I am able to stand before His throne with confidence and boldness in prayer. He truly is high and lifted up and it is His train that fills the temple…not mine.

Maybe you can't imagine that for yourself, but if you have some fight in your belly and you don't know how to use it, you might be an intercessor. If you feel your heart breaking for others, you might be an intercessor. If you weep with compassion, you might be an intercessor. If you can't stop praying for the life of you, you might be an intercession. If you are not scared of the humbling, you might be an intercessor.

Prayer is a beautiful and powerful way to experience the beauty and power of Jesus.

This lifestyle is not for wimps, it is for those who are not afraid of spiritual warfare. To fight things that are unseen in the natural, but so very real in the supernatural.

> "Then said I, Woe is me! for I am undone; because I am a man of unclean lips, and I dwell in the midst of a people of unclean lips: for mine eyes have seen the King, the Lord of hosts. Then flew one of the seraphims unto me, having a live coal in his hand, which he had taken with the tongs from off the altar: And he laid it upon my mouth, and said, Lo, this hath touched thy lips; and thine iniquity is taken away, and thy sin purged. Also I heard the voice of the Lord, saying, Whom shall I send, and who will go for us? Then said I, Here am I; send me" (Isaiah 6:5-8).

Isaiah's repentance and the purging of his sin gave him the confidence to say, "Here am I, send me." This is the ministry of reconciliation that was completed on the cross (2 Corinthians 5:18). Your sins are no more, you are washed in the blood of the Lamb, and ready to go where you are led.

What is reconciliation?
Reconcile means to restore.

My mother always says she has to "reconcile her checkbook," meaning what goes out must line up with what comes in. Everything in our lives must be in good standing with the Lord. It is Jesus' work on the cross that allows for reconciliation, and it is our repentance that reconciles us. Without repentance we have not truly made ourselves right with Jesus. The potential is there, but we have not taken advantage of it.

Jesus goes about constantly trying to draw us into good standing. He says, "You've written some checks you can't pay for. Your account is in the negative. You don't have enough to make it right. Here, let Me reconcile that for you. You were once in debt, but now you are good. Everything is as it should be."

> "Therefore if any man be in Christ, he is a new creature: old things are passed away; behold, all things are become new. And all things are of God, who hath reconciled us to himself by Jesus Christ, and hath given to us the ministry of reconciliation; To wit, that God was in Christ, reconciling the world unto himself, not imputing their trespasses unto them; and hath committed unto us the word of reconciliation. Now then we are ambassadors for Christ, as though God did beseech you by us: we pray you in Christ's stead, be ye reconciled to God. For he hath made him to be sin for us, who knew no sin; that we might be made the righteousness of God in him" (2 Corinthians 5:17-21).

The second time God told Jonah, "Go to Nineveh," he went. There were no ifs, ands, or buts about it. He had been in the belly of the whale and knew the depths of it. He had had an experience and came out praising and willing to go where he was called. Now it is your turn, will you follow the call of repentance and intercession for the lost and the hurting?

BLESSED

"Now the Lord had said unto Abram, Get thee out of thy country, and from thy kindred, and from thy father's house, unto a land that I will shew thee: And I will make of thee a great nation, and I will bless thee, and make thy name great; and thou shalt be a blessing: And I will bless them that bless thee, and curse him that curseth thee: and in thee shall all families of the earth be blessed."

- Genesis 12:1-3

God put a blessing on Abraham. But what is a blessing? Can we have something if we don't understand what it is?

When it comes to being blessed, we can be comforted that it is God who does the blessing. His blessings rest on us. They come down like showers.

Blessed often means being happy and joyful, but not always. Job was blessed. Job who lost his family, his wealth, his good health, and his friends. Job was blessed because God was concerned about him. From the beginning to the end, his story was in God's hands. God allowed certain things in his life. These things had to take place so Job could see the goodness of who his God was and the fullness of who God is, "I have heard of thee by the hearing of the ear: but now mine eye seeth thee" (Job 42:5).

Can we be blessed if we don't see our blessings? Job was blessed at the beginning, he was blessed in the going through, and he was double blessed at the end. Job doubled his wealth, his livestock, his homes, and would go on to have more children. It was more than what he could have imagined for himself in the midst of his despair. Despair does not take away from the blessing, it only multiplies the joy to come.

In the Book of Matthew, Jesus describes who is blessed according to the kingdom of God and what blessing they receive:

> And seeing the multitudes, he went up into a mountain: and when he was set, his disciples came unto him: And he opened his mouth, and taught them, saying, Blessed are the poor in spirit: for theirs is the kingdom of heaven. Blessed are they that mourn: for they shall be comforted. Blessed are the meek: for they shall inherit the earth. Blessed are they which do hunger and thirst after righteousness: for they shall be filled. Blessed are the merciful: for they shall obtain mercy. Blessed are the pure in heart: for they shall see God. Blessed are the peacemakers: for they shall be called the children of God. Blessed are they which are persecuted for righteousness' sake: for theirs is the kingdom of heaven. Blessed are ye, when men shall revile you, and persecute you, and shall say all manner of evil against you falsely, for my sake. Rejoice, and be exceeding glad: for great is your reward in heaven: for so persecuted they the prophets which were before you.
>
> - Matthew 5:1-12

Remember, Jesus is a teacher. Can you imagine this scene? Hundreds, maybe thousands of people watching Jesus. This miracle working Jesus as He makes His way up the mountain- all eyes are on Him. They are waiting in expectancy, listening for what He might say. Then, HE OPENS HIS MOUTH. Have you ever waited for something and then it happened? The people were waiting for their Teacher, then He opened His mouth and began to teach them what it meant to be blessed.

There is an equation to Jesus' teaching. It isn't math, but it is where one thing equals another thing. This equals that.

You will notice from the Beatitudes that the blessing comes after the part we would consider not blessed. The blessing for Abraham came after he was called away from his family into a foreign land. With God there is always an after.

Blessed are the poor in spirit:
for theirs is the kingdom of heaven.

A broken spirit means you are easily moved by the things that move God, "The sacrifices of God are a broken spirit: a broken and a contrite heart, O God, thou wilt not despise" (Psalm 51:17-19).

You are easily driven to prayer.
You are easily driven to repentance.
You don't think of yourself higher than you ought to.
Your heart is tender.
You weep with those who weep.

You rejoice with those who rejoice.

Blessed are they that mourn:
for they shall be comforted.

Mourning in life is inevitable.

People don't live forever, but Jesus says when you must mourn you shall be comforted. Jesus is the comforter. The Holy Ghost was sent to comfort us. This life can be tough, and we need some reassurance. There are a lot of places to find temporary comfort, but true peace can only ever come from Jesus.

Blessed are the meek:
for they shall inherit the earth.

Meek means you are gentle, righteous, humble and teachable. You are quick to listen and slow to speak. You can be bold and be meek. You can be a fire starter and still be meek. Meek is an attitude of submission to God and the things of God. David was out riding when a man started throwing stones at him and cursed him (2 Samuel 16:5-13). David's riding buddy wanted to cut off his head, but David said (to paraphrase), "Let him curse me. If God told him to, then perhaps God will use it to bless me." David could have retaliated, but he chose the better way. He chose to allow wisdom to override pride. He chose to look for the hand of God in that moment. Being meek means that we are easily molded into something stronger because we refuse to let our pride get in the way. The meek shall inherit the earth.

Blessed are they which do hunger and thirst after righteousness:
for they shall be filled.

When our hearts are right, our motives are right. When we want to be right with the Lord, He will fill us up. We will overflow with knowledge, wisdom, truth, love, peace, joy, and every good thing. The Word says God withholds nothing good from His children (Psalm 84:11). When we pray to be right, God will make us right...but again, we must be teachable to be changed.

Blessed are the merciful:
for they shall obtain mercy.

Showing mercy means we are soft when we have every reason to be hard. We are kind when we would be justified to be cruel. When all the evidence points towards pinning someone to the wall, yet we choose to treat them with dignity, then we are being merciful. Giving someone a way out instead of what they deserve reflects the mercy seat of God.

Blessed are the pure in heart:
for they shall see God.

The prayer we have on repeat in our heart is "Create in me a clean heart, O God, and renew a right spirit within me" (Psalm 51:10). A clean heart is made clean through the Word of God. The Word will cleanse all the filth of the world and this flesh, leaving behind room for what is holy. The combination of a clean heart and a renewed spirit will open the windows of heaven and release God's will in earth through you and the works of your hands. The meditations of your heart will manifest through your life, shining bright your Jesus reflection for all to see.

Blessed are the peacemakers:
for they shall be called the children of God.

Peacemakers are the ones who change the atmosphere and the course of relationships. When there is potential for conflict, they choose to forgive and turn the other cheek. When you could "one up" somebody, you choose to be gentle with your words and humble in your actions. Peacemakers understand what it is to be stepped upon for the greater good. They get how Jesus could die for his friends. Peacemakers take on the generational blessing of the Spirit of God in their lives.

Blessed are they which are persecuted for righteousness' sake: for theirs is the kingdom of heaven. Blessed are ye, when men shall revile you, and persecute you, and shall say all manner of evil against you falsely, for my sake. Rejoice, and be exceeding glad: for great is your reward in heaven: for so persecuted they the prophets which were before you.

This is the nuts and bolts of being a Jesus follower. Are you willing to be persecuted for the greater good? To be persecuted means you are willing to:
Be poor in spirit
Mourn
Be meek
Hunger and thirst for righteousness

Be merciful
Refine your heart
Be a peacemaker

Living out the testimony of Jesus is the biggest eternal blessing we can have. It may not look like a blessing, it may not feel like a blessing, but the disciples were beaten and counted it as joy:

> And to him they agreed: and when they had called the apostles, and beaten them, they commanded that they should not speak in the name of Jesus, and let them go. And they departed from the presence of the council, rejoicing that they were counted worthy to suffer shame for his name. And daily in the temple, and in every house, they ceased not to teach and preach Jesus Christ.
>
> -Acts 5:40-42

THE DAY OF VISITATION

"I will declare thy name unto my brethren: in the midst of the congregation will I praise thee. Ye that fear the Lord, praise him; all ye the seed of Jacob, glorify him; and fear him, all ye the seed of Israel. For he hath not despised nor abhorred the affliction of the afflicted; neither hath he hid his face from him; but when he cried unto him, he heard. My praise shall be of thee in the great congregation: I will pay my vows before them that fear him. The meek shall eat and be satisfied: they shall praise the Lord that seek him: your heart shall live for ever. All the ends of the world shall remember and turn unto the Lord: and all the kindreds of the nations shall worship before thee."

- Psalms 22:22-27

Psalms 22:24 tells us Jesus does not despise nor abhor the affliction of the afflicted, meaning the struggles you deal with will never scare Him off. He will not think less of you. He will not hide Himself from what you are going through.

Nothing is too much for Him. You cannot wear Him out. You cannot gross Him out. He will not be disgusted with you and turn His face.

To be afflicted is to suffer. Vine's Bible Dictionary says it is to "undergo a hard substance." We are all afflicted with sin. We have all been maltreated by the enemy. Nobody is immune to adversity. There are struggles we choose and struggles that happen to us. What a blessing to mankind that every living soul knows what it is to be in need of a savior. As far as sin goes, the President of the United States is in no better shape than a beggar on the street. We are all equal in our need for Jesus.

A symbol for being afflicted is a callus. Have you ever had a callus? They aren't very pretty. Calluses are caused from repeated friction, like shoes that rub up against your feet. Your skin tries to protect itself from the cause of the pain, it gets tough, and forms a hard place on your foot. Usually, they develop in places that get used a lot. You don't get many calluses on your face or your arm, but those places of repeat offense, they get callused.

We, the body of Christ, get spiritual calluses. Places that have been afflicted. Offenses that occur over and over again. As a defense mechanism, we make ourselves tough, we think, "if I can just be hard enough, nothing will get through. I will be protected from this affliction."

In Psalm 22, David speaks of his affliction right in the middle of declaring "I will praise you in the midst of the congregation," and "My praise shall be of thee in the great congregation." Affliction lives in-between praise. David said, "He did not despise me, He did not despise my affliction, He did not turn His face from me, but when I cried out to Him, He heard me."

Jesus will hear you in the mess of things. When you are surrounded by miry clay, when the stronghold has its grip, when the offense happens, Jesus will listen for the sound of your voice crying out and He will hear you.

Within your praise, call out to Jesus. Say to Him, "I am afflicted, Jesus. I have an issue, Jesus. I am callused from this world. There is a problem that keeps bothering me. Jesus, will you help me?"

In the Bible we see examples of people running to Jesus with their problems: the woman with the issue of blood, the blind man on the street, and the centurion with his servant. Over and over again we see people cry out to God in the midst of Israel, a congregation who did not know the day of their visitation:

> And when he was come nigh, even now at the descent of the mount of Olives, the whole multitude of the disciples began to rejoice and praise God with a loud voice for all the mighty works that they had seen; Saying, Blessed be the King that cometh in the name of the Lord: peace in heaven, and glory in the highest. And some of the Pharisees from among the multitude said unto him, Master, rebuke thy disciples. And he answered and said unto them, I tell you that, if these should hold their peace, the stones would immediately cry out. And when he was come near, he beheld the city, and wept over it, Saying, If thou hadst known, even thou, at least in this thy day, the things which belong unto thy peace! but now they are hid from thine eyes. For the days shall come upon thee, that thine enemies shall cast a trench about thee, and compass thee round, and keep thee in on every side,
>
> - Luke 19:37-43

Jesus wept over that city. He wept over His people. They missed it. God in flesh had shown up on their doorstep and they wouldn't let Him in.

Some people saw it. There will always be some who fight the crowds and do whatever they have to do to get to Jesus, but as a whole, as a congregation, they missed Jesus as He walked by. Sure, they praised Him, they said, "Blessed be the King," but they didn't call out in their affliction. Their hearts were hardened. They were too worried about rules, who fit in where, who was the best, who had the best seats, who was greeted and who wasn't, who was an outcast and who deserved to be stoned.

God had given them religion to keep them righteous, but they had carried it so far that when God showed up they couldn't see past their own desires. They were too proud to ask for help. They were callused.

Thank God for the ones who cried out. Those brave souls who ran to Jesus are our examples of how to overcome the fear of man and run after the heart of the Lord. Everything man is worried about and what seems right to him is flesh (Proverbs 14:12). We must look higher than the crowd.

> "All the ways of a man are clean in his own eyes; but the Lord weigheth the spirits" (Proverbs 16:2).

One of my favorite examples of crying out is blind Bartimaeus (Mark 10: 46-52). He was on the side of the road, in a group of people, when he heard the Master was coming.

This was his shot at healing. He started to cry out, but everyone around him told him to be quiet. Everyone told him to stop. Bartimaeus had a choice. Would he do what the congregation said to do, or would he yell out and be heard by Jesus?

This blind man knew he only had one choice. If he wanted his healing, he would have to be loud. He would have to go against the normal way of things, and so he did. He cried out to Jesus.

He was heard and then he was healed.

Jesus told the Israelites, "If you had known the things which belong unto thy peace." He prophesied to them that there would be a day when they would be in real affliction from the hands of an enemy. In other words, Jesus was saying, "If you only knew how to cry out now, it could have all been avoided. If you had come to Me in this small affliction, you could have avoided a much larger pain later, but later it will be too late."

When kids are little, they come to you with everything. Every scrape. Every scratch. They want a band aid on everything. This is how we are supposed to be with Jesus, saying "Lord, I need you to heal everything. The little scratches I get throughout my day. The bumps and bruises of my soul." Emotional wounds, physical wounds, whatever the case He gets them all. He will not despise your affliction.

> "Come unto me, all ye that labour and are heavy laden, and I will give you rest. Take my yoke upon you, and learn of me; for I am meek and lowly in heart: and ye shall find rest unto your souls. For my yoke is easy, and my burden is light" (Matthew 11:28-30).

Have you cried out to Jesus lately?

SOLDIER WORDS

"Obey them that have the rule over you and submit yourselves: for they watch for your souls, as they that must give account, that they may do it with joy, and not with grief: for that is unprofitable for you."
-Hebrew 13:17

Authority is a revelation. If you understand authority, you understand the way the Kingdom of God works. Everything in His kingdom responds to the order of authority.

Authority is the right to give orders and make decisions.

Psalms 24:1 says, "The earth is the Lord's, and the fulness thereof; the world, and they that dwell therein." The fullness means everything that is in the earth, seen or unseen belongs to Jesus. He created it and He established it. He gives and He takes away (Job 1:21).

The way we, children of God, advance in the kingdom is by respecting the authority Jesus has over us:
> That at the name of Jesus every knee should bow, of things in heaven, and things in earth, and things under the earth; And that every tongue should confess that Jesus Christ is Lord, to the glory of God the Father.
> - Philippians 2:10-11

When we confess with our mouths that Jesus is Lord it glorifies our God. Like any subject under authority, we submit to who Jesus is and the power He holds. Jesus, however, is not a cruel dictator. He would never force us into agreement, instead He loves us into the kingdom, "Thou hast also given me the shield of thy salvation: and thy right hand hath holden me up, and thy gentleness hath made me great" (Psalm 18:35).

There is a story of a centurion in the book of Matthew who came to Jesus. He was a commander of the Roman Empire who operated under authority and understood how it worked:

> And when Jesus was entered into Capernaum, there came unto him a centurion, beseeching him, And saying, Lord, my servant lieth at home sick of the palsy, grievously tormented. And Jesus saith unto him, I will come and heal him. The centurion answered and said, Lord, I am not worthy that thou shouldest come under my roof: but speak the word only, and my servant shall be healed. For I am a man under authority, having soldiers under me: and I say to this man, Go, and he goeth; and to another, Come, and he cometh; and to my servant, Do this, and he doeth it. When Jesus heard it, he marvelled, and said to them that followed, Verily I say unto you, I have not found so great faith, no, not in Israel.
>
> -Mathew 8:5-10

The centurion basically told Jesus, "I see who You are. I see how You operate. I hear the way You speak and when You speak things happen. I understand authority and since I understand authority, I respect Your authority to heal others. Would You just say the words? If You just speak the words, I know the words will do what You have asked them to do." The Bible says that Jesus' words never return void (Isaiah 55:11).

Imagine a word that is spoken as a soldier. You think that word in your heart or in your mind, and then that very word leaves your mouth. Imagine your body as a tent and this word, this soldier, is told where to go and what to do. Would a soldier who understands authority not do the thing it is ordered to do? *YOU* are responsible for your soldier words. You tell those words what to create in the world. The centurion said, "Just speak the word." He knew the word would obey Jesus, the King of kings and the Lord of lords.

How did Jesus respond to this Roman officer? This non-Jew who was not even supposed to be on His radar because Jesus didn't come for the Romans, He came for the Jews. In the context of revelation, however, Jesus marveled at his faith. He was astonished.

We are used to people being astonished by Jesus, but here Jesus was astonished by a person. He was blown away by his faith. He couldn't believe it! He said, "I've never seen anything like it!"

We need faith that knocks Jesus off His feet.
When He sees you does he marvel?

Our prayer is, "Lord, I believe; help thou mine unbelief" (Mark 9:24). We ask saying, "Lord, I have faith, but help me where I don't. Help me in the places where I can't see what You are doing and my loss of vision leads to a lack of faith. Help me when I don't think You can do it, or I don't think You will do it, or I don't think You want to do it. Lord, I believe; help thou mine unbelief."

There are times when we think our way is the better way. This is called rebellion. When we refuse to recognize and submit to authority we are operating in rebellion.

What are the risks of rebellion?

Saul, who was king before David, lost his throne due to rebellion. Saul was told to take Amelekites in war and destroy everything, but instead he only did part of what God asked him to do. He chose rebellion when he chose to only do part of what was asked of him:

> Wherefore then didst thou not obey the voice of the Lord, but didst fly upon the spoil, and didst evil in the sight of the Lord? And Saul said unto Samuel, Yea, I have obeyed the voice of the Lord, and have gone the way which the Lord sent me, and have brought Agag the king of Amalek, and have utterly destroyed the Amalekites. But the people took of the spoil, sheep and oxen, the chief of the things which should have been utterly destroyed, to sacrifice unto the Lord thy God

in Gilgal. And Samuel said, Hath the Lord as great delight in burnt offerings and sacrifices, as in obeying the voice of the Lord? Behold, to obey is better than sacrifice, and to hearken than the fat of rams. For rebellion is as the sin of witchcraft, and stubbornness is as iniquity and idolatry. Because thou hast rejected the word of the Lord, he hath also rejected thee from being king. And Saul said unto Samuel, I have sinned: for I have transgressed the commandment of the Lord, and thy words: because I feared the people, and obeyed their voice. Now therefore, I pray thee, pardon my sin, and turn again with me, that I may worship the Lord.

-1 Samuel 15:19-25

From here we learn a few things about the heart of God:
Obedience is better than sacrifice.
Rebellion is the same as witchcraft.
Stubbornness is sin and idolatry.

When we reject the Word of the Lord, we reject the call on our life and the will of God. Rebellion is no small thing. Are there any ways you are rebellious against God's word? What has He told you to do that you refuse to do? Give more? Forgive more? Worship more? Let some vices go?

We learn what not to do with Saul and that, "Better is the end of a thing than the beginning thereof: and the patient in spirit is better than the proud in spirit" (Ecclesiastes 7:8).

We must be faithful all the way through, the same way God is faithful to us all the way through. If He suddenly decided to stop, where would we be? We cannot afford to be rebellious.

To whom much is given, much is expected (Luke 12:48). The more He trusts us, the more we are able to do in His kingdom. The more we are able to do, the more obedience is required. We must be obedient in everything, every step of the way. Make sure your faith faileth not. Run the race until the end (2 Timothy 4:7).

The centurion said, "I am a man under authority, having soldiers under me." The only way to grow in the kingdom is to submit to authority. Submit to God and the leaders He has placed in your lives. Maturing in Christ is knowing when and how to submit. My Pastor, Bro. Stacy Lisenbey, preaches the idea of a submissive spirit by saying, "If we agree, then it's not submission."[1] Submission is doing something even if you don't agree with it. Chances are you will mature into agreement. Once you agree and begin to do things out of obedience to the Word, the Lord will grow you up into that understanding. You will start to see things His way because you have grown. This is the same line of thinking that says the weak are strong. When Jesus does a thing, He usually does it in a way that is opposite of how we would do it. Submit to authority and you will be elevated.

---

[1] Bro. Stacy Lisenbey is Pastor at Jesus Name Church in Plainview, Arkansas. www.jesusnamechurch.org

ANATOMY OF THE HEART

"When thou saidst, Seek ye my face; my heart said unto thee, Thy face, Lord, will I seek."

- Psalm 27:8

We are all living out this life as a spiritual experience, much like a fish experiences water, not because the fish chooses the water, but because it is surrounded by water.

You and I are called to navigate the invisible waters of the Spirit in our earthy bodies. Paul called us earthy bodies, not earthly, but earthy, flesh and bone carved from dirt (1 Corinthians 15:47).

Anatomy refers to the human body, but it also means how things are connected, or the infrastructure. Just like our brain must communicate with our feet for us to win the race, the church body must effectively communicate the love of Jesus to win the lost.

There is a type of conversation between us and the Lord that is the gold standard, the premium subscription, it is when God speaks directly to the heart of a person.

Communication between humans is complicated. There are six primary factors in every personal interaction:[2]

---

[2] This is something I learned many years ago while teaching Communications. I was not able to find the original reference but have learned it by heart and am sharing it with you now.

1. Who I am.
2. Who you are.
3. Who you think I am.
4. Who I think that you are.
5. What I said.
6. What you heard me say.

That is a lot of opportunity for us to get it wrong and we get it wrong all the time. For example, I might not really know who you are, the intentions of your heart, or the message you were trying to convey to me. There's a pretty good chance that when two people are upset at one another the problem is a failure to properly send and receive information, emotions, and ideas.

But when the Lord speaks to your heart, it is clear and concise. Such as the sound a tuning fork makes which is said to be a pure noise. When a tuning fork is hit, instruments are put back in rhythm. The sound of it is clear and concise. Psalms 27:8 is our tuning fork with Jesus. In a crazy, strange world where every day feels like a new day, where people are yelling at one another and life seems upside down, we can find peace by getting our hearts back in rhythm, responding to the command, "Seek ye my face." and answering with our hearts, "Thy face Lord will I seek."

I believe what the Jesus is saying to us is, "Open your hearts. There are some hidden things I want to reveal. Some mysteries I want to make known." God moves in the secret places of our hearts.

> "He made darkness his secret place; his pavilion round about him were dark waters and thick clouds of the skies" (Psalm 18:11).

There are levels of communication with the Lord- waves and billows. We like to talk about seasons, but what is even more exciting are stages. Ezekiel 47 measures flood stages at ankles, knees, and loins.

Our walk with Jesus is further in, deeper down, and higher up. It is breadth, length, depth, and height. We need to get used to the shift in altitude. There is an ocean hidden in His heart. We have a supernatural telephone wire tied from our heart to His, or perhaps it is more of an umbilical cord. But here is the question, "Are you able to perceive it?"

The cord may be invisible, but when the phone rings you'll feel the veil rip from top to bottom.

What can you expect from talking to Jesus:

1. God speaks to the heart in a way that heals.

In the aftermath of Jesus' burial, the disciples were devastated. They lost someone they loved. Someone who couldn't be replaced:

> And they talked together of all these things which had happened. And it came to pass, that, while they communed together and reasoned, Jesus himself drew near, and went with them. But their eyes were holden that

they should not know him. And he said unto them, What manner of communications are these that ye have one to another, as ye walk, and are sad…Then he said unto them, O fools, and slow of heart to believe all that the prophets have spoken: Ought not Christ to have suffered these things, and to enter into his glory? And beginning at Moses and all the prophets, he expounded unto them in all the scriptures the things concerning himself. And they drew nigh unto the village, whither they went: and he made as though he would have gone further. But they constrained him, saying, Abide with us: for it is toward evening, and the day is far spent. And he went in to tarry with them. And it came to pass, as he sat at meat with them, he took bread, and blessed it, and brake, and gave to them. And their eyes were opened, and they knew him; and he vanished out of their sight. And they said one to another, Did not our heart burn within us, while he talked with us by the way, and while he opened to us the scriptures?

- Luke 24:14-32

When Jesus showed up the disciples had already talked themselves into a mess. With every "Woe is us" their faith shrank smaller and smaller. They were relying on their own reasoning to cope with their sadness… but then came Jesus. He drew near to them and spoke to their hearts, healing the inner workings of their understanding. He opened up the scriptures and caused a change in anatomy. The disciples asked one another, "Didn't our hearts burn within us?" This wasn't a metaphorical kind of burning, it wasn't heartburn from their dinner, it was the deep work of the Lord in the heart of man. He reaches places only God can reach. He was healing them through His Word. There is a sadness that can only be healed through Jesus. Nothing could replace Jesus for them but Jesus. And I would say if you are dealing with a loss, Jesus can heal that pain for you. His love is like ointment. He packs wounds with His Word. In His presence is the fullness of joy.

2. How we perceive God is how we approach God.

The parable of the talents tells of a man who left money with his servants. He trusted they would be good stewards and that they would bring an increase while he was gone. When the man returned to see what happened while he was away:

> And so he that had received five talents came and brought other five talents, saying, Lord, thou deliveredst unto me five talents: behold, I have gained beside them five talents more. His lord said unto him, Well done, thou good and faithful servant: thou hast been faithful over a few things, I will make thee ruler over many things: enter thou into the joy of thy lord. He also that had received two talents came and said, Lord, thou deliveredst unto me two talents: behold, I have gained two other talents beside them. His lord said unto him, Well done, good and faithful servant; thou

hast been faithful over a few things, I will make thee ruler over many things: enter thou into the joy of thy lord. Then he which had received the one talent came and said, Lord, I knew thee that thou art an hard man, reaping where thou hast not sown, and gathering where thou hast not strawed: And I was afraid, and went and hid thy talent in the earth: lo, there thou hast that is thine. His lord answered and said unto him, Thou wicked and slothful servant, thou knewest that I reap where I sowed not, and gather where I have not strawed: Thou oughtest therefore to have put my money to the exchangers, and then at my coming I should have received mine own with usury. Take therefore the talent from him, and give it unto him which hath ten talents. For unto every one that hath shall be given, and he shall have abundance: but from him that hath not shall be taken away even that which he hath. And cast ye the unprofitable servant into outer darkness: there shall be weeping and gnashing of teeth.

- Matthew 25:20-30

The servants with five and two talents came to the Lord with joy, like a child showing the A+ they made on their report card. They went to the man completely free from fear, they spoke out of excitement at his coming, and in return they were given words of praise and acceptance, "Well done, good and faithful servant."

I like that this parable gives us a pattern. The first servant comes, and everything is good, the second servant comes, and everything is good, but then the third servant gets to the front of the line and there is a problem.

He walked up with an excuse at the ready. He was armed with blame and what he received was wrath. That servant had an unsubmitted gift of knowledge. He said "I knew you were a hard man. I knew you weren't going to help me. I knew you took what wasn't yours to take. You gave me this burden, but I knew you wouldn't help me fulfill it."

How we perceive the Lord is how we approach Him.

The master, however, didn't back down. He said, "If you knew I was such a terrible guy, then at the very least you should have moved out of fear." If you can't move from faith, at the very least you should move from fear. The fear of the Lord is the beginning of wisdom (Proverbs 9:10).

If we do not know God's heart for us, we might wrap this whole thing up and realize we saw Him all wrong.

You are not a burden to God. You are precious in the sight of the Lord:
> For I am the Lord thy God, the Holy One of Israel, thy Saviour: I gave Egypt for thy ransom, Ethiopia and Seba for thee. Since thou wast precious in my sight, thou hast been honourable, and I have loved thee: therefore will I give men for thee, and people

> for thy life. Fear not: for I am with thee: I will bring thy seed from the east, and gather thee from the west; I will say to the north, Give up; and to the south, Keep not back: bring my sons from far, and my daughters from the ends of the earth; Even every one that is called by my name: for I have created him for my glory, I have formed him; yea, I have made him.
>
> -Isaiah 43:3-7

3. Your words reveal your heart

What you say speaks volumes about what is happening on the inside. Your infrastructure is continually being built by your words and is evidenced by your words:

> Do not ye yet understand, that whatsoever entereth in at the mouth goeth into the belly, and is cast out into the draught? But those things which proceed out of the mouth come forth from the heart; and they defile the man. For out of the heart proceed evil thoughts, murders, adulteries, fornications, thefts, false witness, blasphemies: These are the things which defile a man: but to eat with unwashen hands defileth not a man. Then Jesus went thence, and departed into the coasts of Tyre and Sidon.
>
> -Matthew 15:17-21

I like the last bit of these verses that says, "Then Jesus went thence…" which to me sounds like "then Jesus dropped the mic and split."

Our words tell on us. We've all done it. We have all said things we should not have said:

> Among whom also we all had our conversation in times past in the lusts of our flesh, fulfilling the desires of the flesh and of the mind; and were by nature the children of wrath, even as others.".
>
> - Ephesians 2:3

There is Godly conversation and there is conversation that feeds our flesh. It makes us feel good. I'm as guilty as anyone. I used to call it venting, now I call it sin. Have you heard this warning, "Curse not the king, no not in thy thought; and curse not the rich in thy bedchamber: for a bird of the air shall carry the voice, and that which hath wings shall tell the matter" (Ecclesiastes 10:20)?

I don't believe this is a metaphor, or a parable, or any literary device. I think this is a warning that says when you speak out of your flesh your words will travel.

We have to be so mindful about what we say. We have to teach ourselves to do right. The way you change your words is to kill your flesh and purify your heart through prayer and the Word. Our sin nature is too strong on its own. Left to our own devices we are innately sinful, lustful creatures- the Bible says that. The natural thoughts of our heart are wicked:

> Create in me a clean heart, O God; and renew a right spirit within me. Cast me not away from thy presence; and take not thy holy spirit from me. Restore unto me the joy of thy salvation; and uphold me with thy free spirit. Then will I teach transgressors thy ways; and sinners shall be converted unto thee.
>
> - Psalm 51:10-13

Jesus cares about our heart.
He heals us.
He loves us.
He makes us clean.

In these strange times, we must daily realign ourselves to what pleases the Lord.

Simple, concise communication with the One who is:
Holy.
Faithful.
Righteous.
Just.
Sufficient.
Rich in Mercy.
Full of Grace.
Provider.
Protector.
Wonderful.
Blessed.

He's the One who answers all your prayers.
He's the One who cares for you.

He's the One who never leaves you.
He's the One that always takes care of you.
He's the apple of your eye.
He's the lover of your soul.
Our redeemer. Our Savior.

> "When thou saidst, Seek ye my face; my heart said unto thee, Thy face, Lord, will I seek" (Psalm 27:8).

AN APPOINTED TIME

"I will stand upon my watch, and set me upon the tower, and will watch to see what he will say unto me, and what I shall answer when I am reproved. And the Lord answered me, and said, Write the vision, and make it plain upon tables, that he may run that readeth it. For the vision is yet for an appointed time, but at the end it shall speak, and not lie: though it tarry, wait for it; because it will surely come, it will not tarry."
- Habakkuk 2:1-3

In the verses above we see Habakkuk waiting on the Lord. He is watching and listening for a response. He has patiently set his face like flint and girded himself.

When the Lord responds He tells Habakkuk the vision is for an appointed time. When it comes to waiting on Jesus to move there is always an appointed time. Jesus is the timekeeper of our life.

The question is, how are we waiting? Patience, or long-suffering, is a fruit of the Spirit.

To be patient is to accept what is happening without murmuring. To look for God in the waiting. We must choose to be patient. When faced with delay we must stand upon our watch, set upon our tower, and wait for the Lord.

It is hard to wait. Waiting means to deny ourselves. Our human nature says "*NOW*," but God is saying, "There is an appointed time."

The phrase "synchronize your watches" stems from World War I. Action in war had to be precisely scheduled, maneuvers and attacks were timed exactly. The men in the trenches needed watches so they would know how and when to respond. Everyone had to be right on time, not a minute too soon or too late.

There are seasons when our job is to be patient and sit in the trenches of waiting until the timing is right.

> "If a man die, shall he live again? all the days of my appointed time will I wait, till my change come" (Job 14:14).

Job said, "I will wait until my change comes." We will be patient in our faith, knowing our God is able and willing to bring His Word to pass.

While we wait, we aren't sitting around doing nothing. We are praying, learning, and building our faith. We are practicing how to walk in the Spirit of the Lord, how to listen for His voice, and how to watch for His commands:

> But they that wait upon the Lord shall renew their strength; they shall mount up with wings as eagles; they shall run, and not be weary; and they shall walk, and not faint.
> - Isaiah 40:31

How many times have you spoken this scripture over yourself? How many times have you said to yourself, "I am tired of waiting for God, but I know that those who wait shall renew their strength? I know His Word is true. I will keep running and not grow weary. I will walk and not faint. I refuse to give up on God. I will set upon my tower and wait until my change comes." His Word is medicine to a weary soul. His Word gives us the strength to not give up.

When nothing feels like it is changing, you might just be at a gate called beautiful:

> And a certain man lame from his mother's womb was carried, whom they laid daily at the gate of the temple which is called Beautiful, to ask alms of them that entered into the temple; Who seeing Peter and John about to go into the temple asked an alms. And Peter, fastening his eyes upon him with John, said, Look on us. And he gave heed unto them, expecting to receive something of them. Then Peter said, Silver and gold have I none; but such as I have give I thee: In the name of Jesus Christ of Nazareth rise up and walk. And he took him by the right hand, and lifted him up: and immediately his feet and ankle bones received strength. And he leaping up stood, and walked, and entered with them into the temple, walking, and leaping, and praising God. And all the people saw him walking and praising God: And they knew that it was he which sat for alms at the Beautiful gate of the temple: and they were filled with wonder and amazement at that which had happened unto him.
>
> - Acts 3: 2-10

This man was laid daily at the gate called beautiful. Every day the same old gate. The same old ailments. The same old thing, but one day, something different happened. One day he got a miracle. He was asking for money, but he got something better. He got a healing and received a testimony that only God could give him.

> "But let patience have her perfect work, that ye may be perfect and entire, wanting nothing" (James 1:4).

When you and I sit at the gate called beautiful, we will be worked on and tried, but when patience has her perfect work, we will come out in perfect timing. Jesus never leaves anything in the oven too long. He is perfect and everything He does is perfect.

The enemy tells you that God has forgotten about you, but Jesus doesn't forget. He is just waiting for the appointed time.

The enemy tells you God does not care about you, but Jesus loves you. He died for you. You were bought at a price. How could He forget about you?

The enemy tells you God is not able, but nothing is too hard for God.

It isn't Jesus who is lacking, it is only our faith that needs revived. Turn us again, Oh Lord. Renew our faith in You while we wait.

There is an appointed time for every need you have.

BRINGING IN THE SHEAVES

"When the Lord turned again the captivity of Zion, we were like them that dream. Then was our mouth filled with laughter, and our tongue with singing: then said they among the heathen, The Lord hath done great things for them. The Lord hath done great things for us; whereof we are glad. Turn again our captivity, O Lord, as the streams in the south. They that sow in tears shall reap in joy. He that goeth forth and weepeth, bearing precious seed, shall doubtless come again with rejoicing, bringing his sheaves with him."

- Psalm 126:1-6

Psalms 126 describes to us what the joy of deliverance looks like. The author says, "We were like them that dream." Israel had been taken into bondage, but the Lord delivered them out of the clutches of the enemy and now there was laughter and singing. This joy was born from the promise that, "they that sow in tears shall reap in joy." Notice the word says shall. Shall is a promise.

When you take your tears before the Lord and trust Him for the solution, there will eventually be joy.

Here's the process:
Go forth
Weep
Bear your seed
Return rejoicing
Bring your sheaves

Sheaves are bundles of wheat. So, your weeping is the planting and watering of the seed of joy. It doesn't look like joy when it starts, just like a sunflower seed doesn't look like a sunflower. But that joy seed is planted in prayer. It is watered with your faith, and God makes the increase, so that in His timing you can carry your bundle of gladness:

> Through faith also Sara herself received strength to conceive seed, and was delivered of a child when she was past age, because she judged him faithful who had promised.
> -Hebrews 11:11

If you take your tears to your parents, your bestie, or social media, there may or may not be joy at the end. Most likely there will be some form of comfort and hopefully some wisdom, but if you want joy unspeakable and full of glory, then the place you take your crying to is Jesus.

Jesus wants your tears. The woman with the alabaster box brought her crying before the Lord. She wept at His feet, washing them with her tears, drying them with her hair.

Not only do we weep, but Jesus wept:

> Now Jesus was not yet come into the town, but was in that place where Martha met him. The Jews then which were with her in the house, and comforted her, when they saw Mary, that she rose up hastily and went out, followed her, saying, She goeth unto the grave to weep there. Then when Mary was come

> where Jesus was, and saw him, she fell down at his feet, saying unto him, Lord, if thou hadst been here, my brother had not died. When Jesus therefore saw her weeping, and the Jews also weeping which came with her, he groaned in the spirit, and was troubled. And said, Where have ye laid him? They said unto him, Lord, come and see. Jesus wept. Then said the Jews, Behold how he loved him!
>
> - John 11:30-36

I always thought Jesus was weeping for Lazarus, but perhaps the momentum for Jesus' weeping was when He saw Mary weeping, and the Jews weeping. Perhaps He saw them in agony over their loss and then He wept.

Many times our tears have more to do with our burden for other people than for ourselves. When I say burden, I mean that weight we carry for those we love, or specific groups of people that the Lord has placed on our heart. You can carry a burden for people you have never met and will never meet.

Somebody has to carry the burden to prayer.

There is so much in the world to pray about:
Sex trafficking
Child abuse
Poverty
The Lost
Illness

Refugees
Countries in Need
You can love a people you never met. Ask God who He wants you to carry a burden for. Who are you supposed to pray for?

Maybe it's your church.
Maybe it's an outpouring of the Holy Ghost.
God knows what you were born to carry, do you?

Living for God is a rich experience. Living in the Spirit is even richer. When you start paying attention to the invisible, your life becomes a lot more interesting. A life like this means you won't fit into this world so well. You won't be able to watch most movies or read popular books, because most of these are full of sin and offensive to God. Our modern world celebrates sin and puts it on full display. You won't be able to hang out with a lot of people you used to hang out with. You can try but you will be miserable. You won't be able to laugh at things you used to think were funny. They just won't be funny anymore. The good news is you won't want to do those things. You'll get a taste of it and it will taste bad.

Living for Christ means your spirit is used to good food: worship, the Word, Godly fellowship, and a life that is decent and in order. When you taste something ungodly out in the world, you will know. It will feel like you are being poisoned. You will have a reaction. You will have spent too much time in the Word of God for sin to go unnoticed. Give yourself a few weeks without reading your Bible, however, and your sensory perception might start to dim. Those movies will start being funny again and you will laugh at things that hurt God's heart. The enemy will start lying to you and you, being defenseless, might take a bite of that forbidden fruit.

As you walk around in the world and not of the world, carry your sheaves with you, all that weeping that God has turned into joy, praise, and the fruits of the Spirit.

Joseph was sold into slavery by his brothers. That's a pretty big deal. We get mad when our sister steals our sweater or our brother tells us what to do, but Joseph's flesh and blood literally sold him to a people they did not know. They had no idea what would happen to him. They didn't care if he lived or died. If I was Joseph, I would have been pretty upset, maybe even tempted to hold a grudge. I'm sure Joseph cried some tears the years he was a slave and in prison, but what did God do for Joseph? Joseph, the dreamer, was freed from captivity and placed second in the kingdom.

When his brothers eventually came to Egypt, they needed food because of the famine. Joseph could have denied them. He could have let them starve and called it justice, but he didn't because the Lord turned his weeping into joy:

> Then Joseph could not refrain himself before all them that stood by him; and he cried, Cause every man to go out from me. And there stood no man with him, while Joseph made himself known unto his brethren. And he wept aloud: and the Egyptians and the house of Pharaoh heard. And Joseph said unto his brethren, I am Joseph; doth my

father yet live? And his brethren could not answer him; for they were troubled at his presence. And Joseph said unto his brethren, Come near to me, I pray you. And they came near. And he said, I am Joseph your brother, whom ye sold into Egypt. Now therefore be not grieved, nor angry with yourselves, that ye sold me hither: for God did send me before you to preserve life. For these two years hath the famine been in the land: and yet there are five years, in the which there shall neither be earing nor harvest. And God sent me before you to preserve you a posterity in the earth, and to save your lives by a great deliverance. So now it was not you that sent me hither, but God: and he hath made me a father to Pharaoh, and lord of all his house, and a ruler throughout all the land of Egypt. Haste ye, and go up to my father, and say unto him, Thus saith thy son Joseph, God hath made me lord of all Egypt: come down unto me, tarry not: And thou shalt dwell in the land of Goshen, and thou shalt be near unto me, thou, and thy children, and thy children's children, and thy flocks, and thy herds, and all that thou hast: And there will I nourish thee; for yet there are five years of famine; lest thou, and thy household, and all that thou hast, come to poverty.

- Genesis 45:1-11

You may be tempted to hold a grudge against some people who did you wrong, the ones who didn't treat you well and caused you to weep, but take that pain to Jesus. See what He does with it.

Joseph's pain was turned into prosperity. He couldn't get mad at his brothers because the Lord had done such wonderful things for him. In fact, Joseph was so healed by the time he saw them that he was able to say, "It wasn't you that sent me here, it was God."

Take a hold of this Word: "And we know that all things work together for good to them that love God, to them who are the called according to his purpose" (Romans 8:28).

This is a promise. *ALL THINGS.*

Your brother betrayed you? It's going to work to your good.
Your past is sketchy? It's going to work to your good.
Your health isn't the best? It's going to work to your good.
You've made a mistake? It's going to work to your good.

God is going to work all things out for you in a way that benefits your walk with Him.

He will heal relationships.
He will ease hardships.
He will mend pain.

Joseph cried so loudly everyone heard it. I believe it was a spiritual release in the atmosphere. There is a lot of weeping in the Bible. Tears are powerful. Sincere hearts move God. However, there will be a day when there are no more tears. No more crying. No more pain. No more suffering. It will only be joy forever and ever:

> And God shall wipe away all tears from their eyes; and there shall be no more death, neither sorrow, nor crying, neither shall there be any more pain: for the former things are passed away.
>
> - Revelations 21:4

Don't be scared to cry, chances are it is the key to what Jesus wants to accomplish through you. His glory in your life is sewn and watered by the tears you shed.

UNDER NEW MANAGEMENT

"There hath no temptation taken you but such as is common to man: but God is faithful, who will not suffer you to be tempted above that ye are able; but will with the temptation also make a way to escape, that ye may be able to bear it."

-1 Corinthians 10:13

The liberating word of 1 Corinthians 10:13 says, "but God is faithful," and since we know Jesus is faithful, we know everything will work out. He will not allow us to be tempted above what we are capable of resisting, as long as He makes the way out and we look to Him for the exit sign that flashes, "but God is faithful."

Temptation is an invitation to do according to the flesh. The enemy sends out an invite through one of the five senses and asks, "Will you participate? Will you forsake what you know to be right for temporary gratification?" Satan is the author of confusion and wants our body to be in turmoil with our spirit, "For the flesh lusteth against the Spirit, and the Spirit against the flesh: and these are contrary the one to the other: so that ye cannot do the things that ye would (Galatians 5:17)."

The antidote to the flesh is the Spirit, but what does this look like in a real, practical way?

Recently, I drove by a restaurant where there was a sign out front that said, "Under new management." The new owners wanted everyone to know that if you walked into their building things would be different than they used to be. The atmosphere is better. The food is better. The service is better. This place is not like it was. From their sign they were declaring, "We are under new management, expect something different."

When the devil tempts you, simply let him know *"I'M UNDER NEW MANAGEMENT.* Things are not going to be like they used to be. I don't do the same things I used to do. I don't spend time with the same people I used to spend time with. I don't talk the same. I don't respond the same. Expect something different."

The apostle Paul, formerly Saul, had a "New Management" experience. He killed Christians. Lots of them. It was his passion, until he had a life-changing encounter with Jesus. His before and after left him a changed man, he was under new management.

Naturally, the Christians who had been hiding from Paul had a hard time believing he had changed and because of this Paul was in a tricky place. The Jews were mad at him because he switched sides, the Christians didn't trust him yet, and there was Paul, running from one and trying to convince the other.

So, what did Paul do? He didn't sneak off quietly. He got loud about his conversion. He went and preached in the synagogues. He was recklessly bold to the point it threatened his life:

> Then was Saul certain days with the disciples which were at Damascus. And straightway he

preached Christ in the synagogues, that he is the Son of God. But all that heard him were amazed, and said; Is not this he that destroyed them which called on this name in Jerusalem, and came hither for that intent, that he might bring them bound unto the chief priests? But Saul increased the more in strength, and confounded the Jews which dwelt at Damascus, proving that this is very Christ. And after that many days were fulfilled, the Jews took counsel to kill him: But their laying await was known of Saul. And they watched the gates day and night to kill him. Then the disciples took him by night, and let him down by the wall in a basket. And when Saul was come to Jerusalem, he assayed to join himself to the disciples: but they were all afraid of him, and believed not that he was a disciple. But Barnabas took him, and brought him to the apostles, and declared unto them how he had seen the Lord in the way, and that he had spoken to him, and how he had preached boldly at Damascus in the name of Jesus.

- Acts 9:19-27

Paul's boldness saved his bacon. Even though the disciples were unsure of him, they knew enough to help him and aided in his escape by lowering him out of a window. Paul was caught in that in-between place, the wilderness of trying to be different than he was before, but also not yet established in who he would become.

When Jesus changes you, everything in you wants to shout it from the rooftops. Everything in you wants to say, "I'm different!" Sometimes, however, it takes time to build a testimony. Paul had to prove himself.

Barnabas was a friend to Paul during this time and shared his testimony with the disciples. He told them about everything Paul had done and spoke. Barnabas was Paul's way into the ministry. When you build your testimony, it will be one word and one event at a time. Character is developed over time and your character will vouch for you.

People may not believe your change. They may be suspicious of your motives. They may not think you are sincere. They will be waiting for you to prove you haven't changed at all. The devil will come along and try to tempt you back into your old ways like a dog returning to its vomit (Proverbs 26:11). But God, who is faithful, will give you a way out.

When Jesus was in the wilderness right before He started His ministry, the devil came and tried to tempt Him out of God's will. He showed Jesus the riches and glory of this world, offering it to Him on a silver platter. Satan told Him, "If you will worship me, I'll give you anything you want." Jesus, knowing this was the easy way out, resisted the devil and caused him to flee.

As a Christian our ways of escape aren't always through a window, but like Jesus, it is always through the Word of God. Our escape looks more like endurance, submission, wisdom and transformation.

It takes endurance to keep running our race, to not give up by not taking the easy way out and not quitting when it is easier to quit than to press on. Endurance means keeping your eyes focused on the road ahead:

> Blessed is the man that endureth temptation: for when he is tried, he shall receive the crown of life, which the Lord hath promised to them that love him. Let no man say when he is tempted, I am tempted of God: for God cannot be tempted with evil, neither tempteth he any man: But every man is tempted, when he is drawn away of his own lust, and enticed. Then when lust hath conceived, it bringeth forth sin: and sin, when it is finished, bringeth forth death.
>
> - James 1:12-15

When we submit we yield to the power of God. Submit to the authority of the Word of God over your life by saying, "Father, if thou be willing, remove this cup from me: nevertheless not my will, but thine, be done" (Luke 22:42).

When we are wise, we use knowledge in a way that profits us. It is one thing to know something, it is another to utilize the information in a way that profits you:

> Get wisdom, get understanding: forget it not; neither decline from the words of my mouth. Forsake her not, and she shall preserve thee: love her, and she shall keep thee. Wisdom is the principal thing; therefore get wisdom: and with all thy getting get understanding. Exalt

> her, and she shall promote thee: she shall bring thee to honour, when thou dost embrace her. She shall give to thine head an ornament of grace: a crown of glory shall she deliver to thee.
>
> - Proverbs 4:5-9

Vines dictionary tells us transformation is to change the natural disposition and temper of man from a state of enmity to God and his law, into the image of God, or into a disposition and temper conformed to the will of God:

> I am crucified with Christ: nevertheless I live; yet not I, but Christ liveth in me: and the life which I now live in the flesh I live by the faith of the Son of God, who loved me, and gave himself for me.
>
> - Galatians 2:20

This world offers nothing that compares to the love of Christ living in us. The enemy will try to pull us into places we don't want to go. Our flesh will desire things that aren't good for us, but the love of God and Spirit of God will save us from ourselves. He is worth the "no" it takes to resist and the "yes" it takes to follow.

"Remember ye not the former things, neither consider the things of old. Behold, I will do a new thing; now it shall spring forth; shall ye not know it? I will even make a way in the wilderness, and rivers in the desert" (Isaiah 43:18-19).

We are under new management and Jesus is our great escape.

CHILDREN OF THE PROMISE

"Neither, because they are the seed of Abraham, are they all children: but, In Isaac shall thy seed be called. That is, They which are the children of the flesh, these are not the children of God: but the children of the promise are counted for the seed. For this is the word of promise, At this time will I come, and Sara shall have a son."

- Romans 9:7-9

A biblical promise is defined as a gift graciously bestowed, not a pledge secured by negotiation. God's promises are like waking up at Christmas and seeing presents with your name on them, presents you had nothing to do with. You didn't buy them. You didn't wrap them. You didn't write your name on them. It was all done by the hand of God for you, out of His love for you.

Promises wrapped like presents.

The Word tells us there is a difference between the children of the flesh and the children of the promise. Abraham was given a promise by God. Abraham tried to make it happen himself through Hagar, but the promise was supposed to be through Sarah. What happened with Hagar was a work of the flesh, but when God's timing was right, when everything was lined up perfectly, Sarah bore the promise.

Through faith Sarah was able to deliver the promise by judging God as faithful. What does that look like in our lives?

It means when all hope seems lost, you say, "Jesus is faithful." When life looks like a mess, you say, "Jesus is faithful." The days you are disappointed, overwhelmed, and feel forgotten in the wilderness of life, you say, "*BUT* Jesus is faithful."

If you have ever stood before a judge, then you know he or she is the one person who makes the decision. Whatever the judge decides is final. All this evidence is brought before the judge and he or she is the one to say, "this is what is true." The judge holds the gavel.

Hebrews 11:11 is a faith verse about Sarah. We learn that we are judges of God's faithfulness. Each one of us must ask, "Is He faithful?" What a big responsibility! We walk around every day saying either "Yes, God is faithful" or "No, God is not faithful."

When we doubt, we are saying "No, God is not faithful. God can't heal me. God can't protect me. God can't provide for me." Any time we declare that God can't, our faith fails. This, my friends, is pride. The spirit of doubt wants you to tell yourself, "God can't change me because I am too hard to change. God can't heal me because this problem is too big for God. God can't provide for me because my needs are bigger than His supply."

Every situation you encounter is a test of your faithfulness...will you judge God as faithful? When you judge God as faithful in every situation, God is using that moment to build faith in you and through your faith you will develop the strength it takes to deliver the promises over your life.

The only condition to God's promises is faith. Do you believe He is "able to do exceedingly abundantly above all that we ask or think, according to the power that worketh in us" (Ephesians 3:20)?

Is He able to:
heal you
promote you
protect you
provide for you
deliver you
restore you
redeem you
and comfort you,
If you decide He is, then you will find that He who promised you is more than able and more than willing to finish the work He has started.

You are a child of the promise so long as you have the faith to judge Him faithful:
> For who is God save the Lord? or who is a rock save our God? It is God that girdeth me with strength, and maketh my way perfect. He maketh my feet like hinds' feet, and setteth me upon my high places. He teacheth my hands to war, so that a bow of steel is broken by mine arms. Thou hast also given me the shield of thy salvation: and thy right hand hath holden me up, and thy gentleness hath made me great. Thou hast enlarged my steps

under me, that my feet did not slip. I have pursued mine enemies, and overtaken them: neither did I turn again till they were consumed. I have wounded them that they were not able to rise: they are fallen under my feet. For thou hast girded me with strength unto the battle: thou hast subdued under me those that rose up against me. Thou hast also given me the necks of mine enemies; that I might destroy them that hate me. They cried, but there was none to save them: even unto the Lord, but he answered them not. Then did I beat them small as the dust before the wind: I did cast them out as the dirt in the streets.

- Psalm 18:31-42

It is God who makes you great. He gives you the strength you need to overcome the forces of the enemy. Without Jesus, you are fighting an impossible battle, but with Jesus, you will overcome every obstacle. Nothing is too hard for God...*NOTHING*.

You may be in a situation where you think "I have no idea how to make this better. I have no idea how to untie this knot. I am frustrated. I am confused. I am scared," but God knows how. Today, He says to you, "You are a child of the promise. Believe in the One who makes the promise. Judge me faithful. Over and over again, I will not disappoint you. You will not be overtaken. I will not let you down. Judge me faithful."

The Israelites were in the dessert after they were freed from Egypt, God showed them the promise land and they had a choice to make, would they judge God as faithful?

Here is what happened:
> And all the children of Israel murmured against Moses and against Aaron: and the whole congregation said unto them, Would God that we had died in the land of Egypt! or would God we had died in this wilderness! And wherefore hath the Lord brought us unto this land, to fall by the sword, that our wives and our children should be a prey? were it not better for us to return into Egypt? And they said one to another, Let us make a captain, and let us return into Egypt. Then Moses and Aaron fell on their faces before all the assembly of the congregation of the children of Israel. And Joshua the son of Nun, and Caleb the son of Jephunneh, which were of them that searched the land, rent their clothes: And they spake unto all the company of the children of Israel, saying, The land, which we passed through to search it, is an exceeding good land. If the Lord delight in us, then he will bring us into this land, and give it us; a land which floweth with milk and honey. Only rebel not ye against the Lord, neither fear ye the people of the land; for they are bread for us: their defence is departed from them, and the Lord is with us: fear them not. But all the congregation bade stone them with stones. And the glory of the Lord appeared in the tabernacle of the congregation before all the children of Israel. And the Lord said unto Moses, How long will this

> people provoke me? and how long will it be ere they believe me, for all the signs which I have shewed among them? I will smite them with the pestilence, and disinherit them, and will make of thee a greater nation and mightier than they.
>
> - Numbers 14:2-12

The Israelites did not judge God as faithful. They did not believe He was going to provide for them or protect them. Their unbelief gave birth to a rebellious spirit. They appointed a new leader. They desired to go back into bondage. At that moment, they became children of the flesh.

There were some who believed God. Caleb, Joshua, Moses, and Aaron still believed in the Lord, but the rest were happy to call God a liar.

In His anger at the Israelites, God was going to destroy them, wipe them off the face of the planet, but Moses interceded. He prayed for them, begged God for their life:

> Pardon, I beseech thee, the iniquity of this people according unto the greatness of thy mercy, and as thou hast forgiven this people, from Egypt even until now. And the Lord said, I have pardoned according to thy word: But as truly as I live, all the earth shall be filled with the glory of the Lord. Because all those men which have seen my glory, and my miracles, which I did in Egypt and in the wilderness, and have tempted me now these ten times, and have not hearkened to my voice; Surely they shall not see the land which I sware unto their

> fathers, neither shall any of them that provoked me see it: But my servant Caleb, because he had another spirit with him, and hath followed me fully, him will I bring into the land whereinto he went; and his seed shall possess it.
>
> - Numbers 14:19-24

The Lord honored Moses' prayer for the people he was called to lead, but He also said, "They will never see the Promise Land, except Caleb, because Caleb has another spirit about him (Numbers 14:30)." The Israelites were children of the flesh, but Caleb was a child of the promise. He judged God as faithful.

Today and every day for the rest of your life you are called to wake up, open your eyes, and declare God as faithful. Are you a child of the flesh or a child of the promise? You get to choose.

Perhaps you are thinking to yourself, "How can I trust someone I don't know?" That is a fair question. It is hard to trust somebody you don't know very well, especially in the world we live in. It takes time to build a relationship.

My answer to you would be, trust Him like a child. Go back to the days before other people misused your trust:

> Whosoever therefore shall humble himself as this little child, the same is greatest in the kingdom of heaven. And whoso shall receive one such little child in my name receiveth me. But whoso shall offend one of these little

ones which believe in me, it were better for him that a millstone were hanged about his neck, and that he were drowned in the depth of the sea.

- Matthew 18: 4-6

Caleb believed God like a little child following behind his father. You and I are little children who wake up every day saying, "God is faithful."

Jesus will:
heal you
promote you
protect you
provide for you
deliver you
restore you
redeem you
and comfort you.

You are children of the promise.

COME UP HIGHER

"But godliness with contentment is great gain. For we brought nothing into this world, and it is certain we can carry nothing out. And having food and raiment let us be therewith content. But they that will be rich fall into temptation and a snare, and into many foolish and hurtful lusts, which drown men in destruction and perdition. For the love of money is the root of all evil: which while some coveted after, they have erred from the faith, and pierced themselves through with many sorrows. But thou, O man of God, flee these things; and follow after righteousness, godliness, faith, love, patience, meekness. Fight the good fight of faith, lay hold on eternal life, whereunto thou art also called, and hast professed a good profession before many witnesses."

-1 Timothy 6:6-12

"Therefore take no thought, saying, What shall we eat? or, What shall we drink? or, Wherewithal shall we be clothed? (For after all these things do the Gentiles seek:) for your heavenly Father knoweth that ye have need of all these things. But seek ye first the kingdom of God, and his righteousness; and all these things shall be added unto you. Take therefore no thought for the morrow: for the morrow shall take thought for the things of itself. Sufficient unto the day is the evil thereof."

- Matthew 6:31-34

These two passages of Scripture tell us what to flee and what to seek. We flee from the worry and lust of worldly possessions; we seek God's righteousness.

What is righteousness?

Righteousness is a gift from God that brings us into right alignment with His Word. Righteousness is not a checklist but a covering.

There is something about us that wants a checklist. I love checklists. I love to scratch things off and feel accomplished, as though I have done something right. It is good to do good works. James 2:20 tells us faith without works is dead, but what about those times it seems as though your works are not enough? You are certain you are wrong in what you do, what you say, and how you feel. What if you are trying to follow God as best as you know how and yet you still feel like a failure? The problem isn't with the checklist, it's with the covering.[3] What have you covered yourself in? His righteousness or yours? Jesus is the only One who can make us right:

> And I saw heaven opened, and behold a white horse; and he that sat upon him was called Faithful and True, and in righteousness he doth judge and make war. His eyes were as a flame of fire, and on his head were many crowns; and he had a name written, that no man knew, but he himself. And he was clothed with a vesture dipped in blood: and his name is called The Word of God.
> - Revelation 19:11-13

---

[3] This message sprang from a conversation with Sis. Peggy Foster who ministered to me about the covering of righteousness.

John describes to us a vision of Jesus on His white horse in all His splendid righteousness, with crowns on His head and a vesture dipped in blood, perhaps the blood that purchased our sins. The vesture He wears is that of a priest because Jesus is our High Priest. He is our covering. We are to seek His righteousness because in His righteousness and His blood we are justified. We were bought at a price, and we are cherished. Jesus took us back from the gates of hell.

He is victor over our lives:
> Knowing that a man is not justified by the works of the law, but by the faith of Jesus Christ, even we have believed in Jesus Christ, that we might be justified by the faith of Christ, and not by the works of the law: for by the works of the law shall no flesh be justified.
> - Galatians 2:16

It is our faith in Jesus that justifies us. We know He *can* do it because He has *already* done it. Our belief in His ability is the catalyst to our covering Abraham was given his own vision of the Lord's ability to cover His promises:
> After these things the word of the Lord came unto Abram in a vision, saying, Fear not, Abram: I am thy shield, and thy exceeding great reward. And Abram said, Lord God, what wilt thou give me, seeing I go childless, and the steward of my house is this Eliezer of Damascus? And Abram said, Behold, to me thou hast given no seed: and, lo, one born in my house is mine heir. And, behold, the word of the Lord came unto him, saying, This

> shall not be thine heir; but he that shall come forth out of thine own bowels shall be thine heir. And he brought him forth abroad, and said, Look now toward heaven, and tell the stars, if thou be able to number them: and he said unto him, So shall thy seed be. And he believed in the Lord; and he counted it to him for righteousness.
>
> - Genesis 15:1-6

Abraham believed in the Lord and that was enough. God counted it to him for righteousness. Abraham believed God therefore God said, "You and I are right."

We have scripture that tells us how to demonstrate our belief. How to be covered in the name of Jesus. To be buried in the waters of baptism and risen with Christ. How to receive the gift of the Holy Ghost:

> Then Peter said unto them, Repent, and be baptized every one of you in the name of Jesus Christ for the remission of sins, and ye shall receive the gift of the Holy Ghost.
>
> -Acts 2:38

We follow this command in obedience to the Word of God. Abraham didn't have the book of Acts. He was there at the first, after Noah and before Moses. But before Abraham was, Jesus said, "I AM" (John 8:58).

You and I are part of that faith promise God made. We have been grafted in by the blood of the lamb.

> "And these all, having obtained a good report through faith, received not the promise: God having provided some better thing for us, that they without us should not be made perfect" (Hebrews 11:39-40).

Faith is defined as "the substance of things hoped for, the evidence of things not seen" (Hebrews 11:1).

Abraham had faith in who God was. He believed Him. He couldn't see his promises at first, but He could see the evidence of who God was. The multitude of the stars. The magnitude of the heavens. In that moment when the Lord said, "Look now toward heaven," He was directing Abraham towards something higher. A higher vision. A higher faith.

Here is John's vision. The beckoning of a higher revelation with Jesus. The call to see more than he had seen before, to believe more than he had believed before. The Lord wanted more for John, and He wants more for you. That same call applies to you. Look at the stars. Come up higher:

> After this I looked, and, behold, a door was opened in heaven: and the first voice which I heard was as it were of a trumpet talking with me; which said, Come up hither, and I will shew thee things which must be hereafter. And immediately I was in the spirit: and, behold, a throne was set in heaven, and one sat on the throne. And he that sat was to look upon like a jasper and a sardine stone: and there was a rainbow round about the throne, in sight like unto an emerald. And round

about the throne were four and twenty seats: and upon the seats I saw four and twenty elders sitting, clothed in white raiment; and they had on their heads crowns of gold. And out of the throne proceeded lightnings and thunderings and voices: and there were seven lamps of fire burning before the throne, which are the seven Spirits of God. And before the throne there was a sea of glass like unto crystal: and in the midst of the throne, and round about the throne, were four beasts full of eyes before and behind. And the first beast was like a lion, and the second beast like a calf, and the third beast had a face as a man, and the fourth beast was like a flying eagle. And the four beasts had each of them six wings about him; and they were full of eyes within: and they rest not day and night, saying, Holy, holy, holy, Lord God Almighty, which was, and is, and is to come. And when those beasts give glory and honour and thanks to him that sat on the throne, who liveth for ever and ever, The four and twenty elders fall down before him that sat on the throne, and worship him that liveth for ever and ever, and cast their crowns before the throne, saying, Thou art worthy, O Lord, to receive glory and honour and power: for thou hast created all things, and for thy pleasure they are and were created.

- Revelation 4:1-11

ESTABLISHED

"Except the Lord build the house, they labour in vain that build it: except the Lord keep the city, the watchman waketh but in vain."

-Psalm 127:1

"I counsel thee to buy of me gold tried in the fire, that thou mayest be rich; and white raiment, that thou mayest be clothed, and that the shame of thy nakedness do not appear; and anoint thine eyes with eyesalve, that thou mayest see."

- Revelation 3:18

If you could choose any profession, what would it be?

When God planned out His time here on earth as Jesus, 100% God, 100% man, He chose to make Himself a carpenter. Joseph, His earthly father, was a carpenter. He came from a family of carpenters, people who built things with their hands. They took a piece of lumber and created exactly what was needed. A table. A chair. A home. An altar. When you are a builder, your material is a blank slate. When you have the skills to build, anything is possible.

Jesus is our Master Builder. We are individual buildings not only designed by Him but built by Him, like when a bricklayer adds bricks to a home. Piece by piece He decides how we are made and what we will be made into:

> For through him we both have access by one Spirit unto the Father. Now therefore ye are no more strangers and foreigners, but fellow

> citizens with the saints, and of the household of God; And are built upon the foundation of the apostles and prophets, Jesus Christ himself being the chief corner stone; In whom all the building fitly framed together groweth unto an holy temple in the Lord: In whom ye also are builded together for an habitation of God through the Spirit.
>
> - Ephesians 2:18-22

The way God works is so beautiful. He builds you exactly as He wants you through the work of His Spirit in you. The way you are built fits perfectly with the way your brothers and sisters are built, so that together the body of Christ is complete. See, Jesus is so wonderful, so powerful, and so special that not one of us could fully be Him, but He called us to be a part of His body. There is something magnificent about being a part of something and needing each other.

We have this human tendency to want to do things all on our own. We like being independent. If we are independent, then we don't have to rely on anyone else. We don't have to risk being let down or disappointed. We hold all the cards and have all the power. We think, "If I can do it on my own, then I know it will be done exactly as I want it done," but this isn't how God built us. He built us to need each other. He established us this way.

After a house sits for a while, it settles. The walls start to crack. The floor can slant. The house has gotten used to being where it is and the weak places begin to show. Today,

God is asking you not to settle. Don't settle for what you have. Keep allowing Him to build you up. You fit well with others in the body of Christ. We need to make room in our lives to grow together. He placed us here as a family, because iron sharpens iron (Proverbs 27:17). Don't labor in vain, instead build others up.

We don't settle in the Lord; we are established in Christ.

To be established is to be confirmed in the place you are planted, but it is also a place of growth and movement. Settled is fine if you don't plan on going anywhere but established is built upwards and rooted downwards.

There are ways, building blocks, that God uses to establish us:

1. Righteousness

"In righteousness shalt thou be established: thou shalt be far from oppression; for thou shalt not fear: and from terror; for it shall not come near thee" (Isaiah 54:14).

This means to choose right and forsake evil. Jesus grew up eating butter and honey so He would know to choose right (Isaiah 7:15). We must turn away from our sinful ways and do things God's ways. If we do this, we will be established. We will be rooted in His love. There is always God's way and the world's way. We must choose what is right.

2. Wisdom

"Through wisdom is an house builded; and by understanding it is established" (Proverbs 24:3).

Wisdom is the knowledge and ability to make right choices regarding God's will. Wisdom is righteousness in action. There is a spirit of wisdom that comes from God. You can pray specifically for wisdom. Read the book of Proverbs and ask God to gift you with the spirit of wisdom so you will be established.

3. Your Works

"Commit thy works unto the Lord, and thy thoughts shall be established" (Proverbs 16:3).

Keep your hands out of the cookie jar. Do everything unto the Lord. Be mindful of your actions. When you are doings something that is an old habit, ask God to take that habit away from you. He will work the old man out of you and establish the new. We develop coping mechanisms in this life, pre-Jesus. Our new man walks in the Spirit, but our old man walked in the flesh. The flesh must cope with itself, so it becomes defensive, it steals, it lies, it manipulates. It is impossible to please God in your flesh. Ask Jesus to teach you how to walk in the Spirit.

4. Your Words

"The lip of truth shall be established for ever: but a lying tongue is but for a moment" (Proverbs 12:19).

Our words build up and they tear down. They build God's will in our life, or they open the gate for the enemy to come and take what isn't his. How we talk to ourselves matters. How we talk to others matters. Your words will go before you. They will establish you. Are you an encourager or do you judge others and tear them down? The choice is yours. Do you want to be like Jesus? Speak like Jesus? Get in His Word. Allow His words to live in you, they will take root in your heart and come out in your conversations, "Thou shalt also decree a thing, and it shall be established unto thee: and the light shall shine upon thy ways" (Job 22:28).

Submit your words to God and He will teach you the right way to speak.

5. Your Testimony

"For he established a testimony in Jacob, and appointed a law in Israel, which he commanded our fathers, that they should make them known to their children" (Psalms 78:5).

What God has done in your life speaks for itself. Your testimony is His testimony: death, burial, resurrection. He is establishing something in you. He has saved you for His name's sake. His name is on your forehead. You aren't in this by yourself. Nobody ever started to build a house then just left it to rot. Jesus is developing your testimony, "Being confident of this very thing, that he which hath begun a good work in you will perform it until the day of Jesus Christ" (Philippians 1:6).

Jesus will do all the heavy lifting. He will purchase all the supplies. He has the blueprint and a vision for what He is building in you, all you have to do is submit. Try saying, "I'm all yours Jesus. Whatever you want, I'll do. I have no other desires in my life than to do what You have planned for me. There is nothing I want except Your will to be done in my life."

The exciting part of this is that Jesus is the Master Builder. He will build a life for you that is beautiful, exciting, and fulfilling. It's going to be wonderful. Every gift you have will be put to use. All your passions will find a home.

Let the Lord establish you. Find out what His plan is. It will be way better than anything you could have imagined for yourself.

> "For I know the thoughts that I think toward you, saith the Lord, thoughts of peace, and not of evil, to give you an expected end" (Jeremiah 29:11).
>
> "And David perceived that the Lord had established him king over Israel, and that he had exalted his kingdom for his people Israel's sake" (2 Samuel 5:12).

EVERY PRECIOUS THING

"He cutteth out rivers among the rocks; and his eye seeth every precious thing."

-Job 28:10-12

Precious isn't a word we use very much with adults, but we will learn that the Lord looks at us as precious to Him and what He gives to us is precious.

Something that is precious is:
1. Of great price
2. Of great value or worth; very valuable.

For something to be precious it must be worth something and cost you something, not everything is precious.

What is precious to you?

If you were stranded on a desert island and could only have one thing, what would it be?

The apostle John found himself stranded on an island, and what was precious to him was what he had within him, the Spirit of God. He said, "I was in the Spirit on the Lord's Day, and heard behind me a great voice, as of a trumpet," (Revelation 1:10).

John would not have traded that experience for anything in the world. I'm sure if you asked him "John, would you rather be at home, eating a steak, surround by your things with the comfort of your Netflix, *or* be abandoned on an island to die, having church by yourself in a cave when the Spirit of the Lord takes you into the heavens and reveals to you the mysteries of God?"

Which do you think he would choose?
What would you choose?
Are the things of God precious to you?

The first thing we need to understand is that we are precious in the eyes of God...We were costly. We are valuable.

Read the Lord's Word for you:
> But now thus saith the Lord that created thee, O Jacob, and he that formed thee, O Israel, Fear not: for I have redeemed thee, I have called thee by thy name; thou art mine. When thou passest through the waters, I will be with thee; and through the rivers, they shall not overflow thee: when thou walkest through the fire, thou shalt not be burned; neither shall the flame kindle upon thee. For I am the Lord thy God, the Holy One of Israel, thy Saviour: I gave Egypt for thy ransom, Ethiopia and Seba for thee. Since thou wast precious in my sight, thou hast been honourable, and I have loved thee: therefore will I give men for thee, and people for thy life. Fear not: for I am with thee: I will bring thy seed from the east, and gather thee from the west; I will say to the north, Give up; and to the south, Keep not back: bring my sons from far, and my daughters from the ends of the earth; Even every one that is called by my name: for I have

created him for my glory, I have formed him; yea, I have made him. Bring forth the blind people that have eyes, and the deaf that have ears.

- Isaiah 43:1-8

Jesus says, "I paid a high price for you. You cost me something." Calvary wasn't cheap but the blood is enough.

The saving gospel of Jesus Christ says you are worthy because He says you are. The lamb of God that taketh away the sins of man, looks at you and says "Worth it." Out part is to look at Him and say "Worthy."

> "And I beheld, and I heard the voice of many angels round about the throne and the beasts and the elders: and the number of them was ten thousand times ten thousand, and thousands of thousands; Saying with a loud voice, Worthy is the Lamb that was slain to receive power, and riches, and wisdom, and strength, and honour, and glory, and blessing" (Revelation 5:11-12).

Jesus is worthy to receive power, riches, wisdom, strength, honour, glory, and blessing.

Do we honour Jesus and the price He paid for our salvation? Do we give Him glory for the good He does in heaven and on earth? Do we bless His name with praise and thanksgiving? We were worth it, but *HE* is worthy. Do we consider the Gospel at work in our lives as a precious commodity to be cherished above all else?

What you carry in the Lord is valuable. Here are some of the riches you have been given in Christ:

1. Jesus

"Wherefore also it is contained in the scripture, Behold, I lay in Sion a chief corner stone, elect, precious: and he that believeth on him shall not be confounded" (Peter-1 2:6).

That chief cornerstone in our lives is Jesus. Without the cornerstone the building cannot stand. It will crumble to the ground. Let us not take Jesus for granted. He is high and lifted up. He is revered. His name is above all other names. There is no God like our God.

2. The Blood of Jesus

"But with the precious blood of Christ, as of a lamb without blemish and without spot" (Peter-1 1:19).

We are saved through the blood of Jesus and only the blood of Jesus. If it were not for the blood, we could never overcome our sins. There would be no way out for us because we could not make enough sacrifices. If we had to sacrifice sheep and goats, they wouldn't be able to keep up with the demand. There is too much sin for us to make it right on our own. The only redemption possible for us is through the blood of Jesus. It is more valuable than anything we could ever hope to own and more costly than anything we could give.

3. Faith

"That the trial of your faith, being much more precious than of gold that perisheth, though it be tried with fire, might be found unto praise and honour and glory at the appearing of Jesus Christ:" (Peter-1 1:7).

Your trials are precious because they increase your faith. What you go through is not in vain. Peter walked on water going after Jesus, but fear go the best of him and he slipped. If he would have just looked back up and fixed his eyes on the Lord, he would have made it all the way across. The strengthening of your inner man is worth more than money could put a price on. We may be poor pilgrims just passing through, but we are rich in our God. What He gives us can't be measured this side of eternity.

4. Worship

"There came unto him a woman having an alabaster box of very precious ointment, and poured it on his head, as he sat at meat" (Matthew 26:7).

Your worship means something to Jesus. When you pour yourself out to the extent of all you have, when you give that last mite to the glory of God, when you leave His house empty, God says "Precious." Why would you hold back when Jesus paid it all? Why would you refrain when God gave all of Himself? Who are you to withhold your worship? Is He not worthy? Is there not a cause? Worshippers arise. When you give all of yourself, you can die knowing you gave it all.

5. God's Promises

"Whereby are given unto us exceeding great and precious promises: that by these ye might be partakers of the divine nature, having escaped the corruption that is in the world through lust" (Peter-2 1:4).

The promises of God keep you on the right path. He tells us what is ahead because He knows if we are hungry for righteousness, it will keep us fed. We will escape the corruption of this world when we settle in ourselves that this world holds no value to us. The only thing that can fulfill us is what God says, what pleases Him, what is lovely in His sight. When He speaks over us, WE turn to Him and say "Precious."

6. Eternal Life

"And the foundations of the wall of the city [were] garnished with all manner of precious stones. The first foundation [was] jasper; the second, sapphire; the third, a chalcedony; the fourth, an emerald" (Revelations 21:19).

At the end of this race there is either a reward or a punishment. Either the greatest joy we could ever know or the greatest torment we could ever experience. The first foundation of heaven is full of precious stones. Beautiful stones that shine and shimmer in the light of Jesus. There will be no more sun, because His light is enough. Natural things will pass away and eternal things will be our new normal. This world holds nothing for us.

Here is the kicker, for a little while we are in this world and must contend with this world. We must keep our crown and finish the race strong. There is wisdom in how to run.

Runners move their arms a certain way. Their legs move to a certain timing. Their inhales and exhales are precise. They are not haphazard. They are in it to win it.

Survival tip:
Don't share your precious things with just anyone.

You are valuable in the sight of the Lord. Your testimony is valuable. The work Jesus is doing in you is valuable. Sometimes we have to keep valuable things under lock and key. We have to be mindful about who we share what with. I'm not talking about witnessing, share the gospel of Jesus as much and as freely as you have the opportunity to do so, but Matthew 7:6 says, "Give not that which is holy unto the dogs, neither cast ye your pearls before swine, lest they trample them under their feet, and turn again and rend you." Healing, revelation, supernatural experiences in Christ, these are things that are sometimes best left in an incubator until the timing is right. Chicks hatch when they are left hidden under the protection of their mother's wing.

The book of Isaiah tells us of King Hezekiah who had great wealth, a palace full of precious things. Hezekiah was not choosy about who he showed his valuables to. The King of Babylon came by and Hezekiah invited him in:

> And Hezekiah was glad of them, and showed

> them the house of his precious things, the silver, and the gold, and the spices, and the precious ointment, and all the house of his armour, and all that was found in his treasures: there was nothing in his house, nor in all his dominion, that Hezekiah showed them not.
>
> - Isaiah 39:2

Instead of going into the lion's den, Hezekiah invited the lions into his house. He did not act in wisdom, and he is our warning about treating precious things as though they are not. We cannot get so used to the things of God that we get sloppy about it.

> "Then said Isaiah to Hezekiah, Hear the word of the Lord of hosts: Behold, the days come, that all that is in thine house, and that which thy fathers have laid up in store until this day, shall be carried to Babylon: nothing shall be left, saith the Lord" (Isaiah 39:5-6).

There is a reason God shuts doors on relationships. Don't invite the enemy in and give him a tour of the precious and necessary work God is doing in your life. Give it time. Wait until the storm passes and the healing is done to pick up the phone. Wait until you are restored and can operate out of a healthy place before you decide to give your testimony. Wait on the Lord to direct your path. He will put you in front of kings in palaces to proclaim the good news of Jesus Christ, don't go about it too early. Don't tear down your own house.

Be wise in the restoration and you won't have to fight old battles in a new place.

God sees you as a fight worth fighting for. A child worth dying for. The enemy of your soul wants you to feel cheap. He says, "You are a dime a dozen. Nobody would miss you if you left. You are easily replaced." This is a lie. Don't believe these words. Don't let them in.

Choose the truth the cross offers. Choose to believe Jesus when He says you are precious.

GLORY, HONOUR & POWER

"And the whole congregation of the children of Israel murmured against Moses and Aaron in the wilderness: 3And the children of Israel said unto them, Would to God we had died by the hand of the Lord in the land of Egypt, when we sat by the flesh pots, and when we did eat bread to the full; for ye have brought us forth into this wilderness, to kill this whole assembly with hunger. Then said the Lord unto Moses, Behold, I will rain bread from heaven for you; and the people shall go out and gather a certain rate every day, that I may prove them, whether they will walk in my law, or no. And it shall come to pass, that on the sixth day they shall prepare that which they bring in; and it shall be twice as much as they gather daily. And Moses and Aaron said unto all the children of Israel, At even, then ye shall know that the Lord hath brought you out from the land of Egypt:"

- Exodus 16: 3-6

This passage in Exodus tells us the response of the children of Israel as they were being led through the wilderness. They murmured and complained against Moses and Aaron, the leaders God put before them. They were grumpy (today we call it hangry) and they did not appreciate the miracles God had already done in their lives. All they could remember were the good things about Egypt, but in Egypt they had been slaves. Forced into hard labor, their freedom completely taken from them, and now here they were, free in the Lord, and all they could think about was the food they used to eat.

They became very dramatic in their complaining.

They said things like, "I wish God would have just let us die. It would have been better to die as slaves than to live like this."

We live in a drama-loving world. Our highs are very high, and our lows are very low. We are a society of Chicken Littles always waiting for the sky to fall and then wonder why things are always happening to us.

The Israelites were, however, in a tough spot. A spiritual wilderness. The place of in-between. They weren't the slaves they used to be, but they also weren't living in the Promise Land. In their discomfort they decided it was everyone's fault but theirs. Instead of embracing where God had them and was leading them, they looked to their past for answers and blamed others as they walked. They said it was God who neglected them. They said it was Moses and Aaron who got them in a mess. They stopped calling their freedom a miracle and started calling it a mess. They loved their lives too much and they did not want to sacrifice to get where they were supposed to be.

Their complaining had become a habit.

Habits are also called tendencies- things we tend to do.

Habits have three parts to them: First, is the trigger, something that throws your brain into an automatic response. Next, is the behavior itself. And finally, the reward.

In the spiritual, we call these strongholds. Automatic patterns of thinking and doing that the Enemy or our flesh has sown into our lives to get a hold of us. Unless we purposely come against them with the Word of God, they will continue operating in our lives until we die.

As the Israelites walked around the dessert, discomfort was their trigger. They were hungry, thirsty, tired, and uncomfortable which triggered the complaining

Then, the reward. Complaining feels good to our flesh. Backbiting makes us feel good. The Bible puts backbiters in the same group as other sinners:

> And even as they did not like to retain God in their knowledge, God gave them over to a reprobate mind, to do those things which are not convenient; Being filled with all unrighteousness, fornication, wickedness, covetousness, maliciousness; full of envy, murder, debate, deceit, malignity; whisperers, Backbiters, haters of God, despiteful, proud, boasters, inventors of evil things, disobedient to parents, Without understanding, covenant breakers, without natural affection, implacable, unmerciful: Who knowing the judgment of God, that they which commit such things are worthy of death, not only do the same, but have pleasure in them that do them.
> - Romans 1:28-32

We are all guilty of not keeping a watch over our mouths. It is up to us to submit our words to Jesus, "Set a watch, O Lord, before my mouth; keep the door of my lips" (Psalm 141:3).

How does God change the way we speak? By changing our heart. Our words are the overflow of our heart. Who could complain when the joy of the Lord overflows within us?

Now, this is easy to say, but much harder to do when you are in the midst of a situation that is tough. Those triggers start going off. The politician you don't like is on tv. Some guy cuts you off in the parking lot. The waitress is rude to you. You are frustrated with the leaders in your life. All of these things are triggers. We must stop the power of the trigger. Change what we used to do into what we do now.

> "I beseech you therefore, brethren, by the mercies of God, that ye present your bodies a living sacrifice, holy, acceptable unto God, which is your reasonable service. And be not conformed to this world: but be ye transformed by the renewing of your mind, that ye may prove what is that good, and acceptable, and perfect, will of God" (Romans 12:1-2).

Our mouths are a part of our body. Our words are the product of our heart- a part of the body. Our voice comes from our throat- a part of the body. Your words are so much a part of you that you cannot separate yourself from them. Jesus says we will be held accountable for every word, "But I say unto you, That every idle word that men shall speak, they shall give account thereof in the day of judgment" (Matthew 12:36).

Honestly, I am not looking forward to the moment I will stand in front of Jesus and hear a replay of every word that I have spoken just for the sake of speaking. The times I lost my temper. The times I was ugly about someone. The times I just let words fly out of my mouth as though they were nothing. Gratefully, however, I have this knowledge now, so I am able to repent and ask forgiveness for every idle word. I plead the blood of Jesus over Every. Idle. Word. I need those words and those conversations to be drenched in the sacrifice of Jesus. That is the only way I will be able to stand in front of Him unashamed. That is the only way I am justified.

What is the best use of our words?

Our words are best used to glorify God. To speak of His goodness. His faithfulness. To testify of His mercy.

We get a taste of this in Revelation:

> And the first beast was like a lion, and the second beast like a calf, and the third beast had a face as a man, and the fourth beast was like a flying eagle. And the four beasts had each of them six wings about him; and they were full of eyes within: and they rest not day and night, saying, Holy, holy, holy, Lord God Almighty, which was, and is, and is to come. And when those beasts give glory and honour and thanks to him that sat on the throne, who liveth for ever and ever, The four and twenty elders fall down before him that sat on the throne, and worship him that liveth for ever and ever, and cast their crowns before the throne, saying, Thou art worthy, O Lord, to receive glory and honour and power: for thou

hast created all things, and for thy pleasure they are and were created.

-Revelation 4:7-11

This scene is one of worship before the throne of Jesus. One day, if we all make heaven, we will worship before the throne of Jesus. Right now, at this very moment, *those beasts* are worshipping God almighty, maker of Heaven and Earth, the was and is and is to come, the author of our salvation, the finisher of our faith. Even now when *those beasts* stand before the Lion of Judah, they can't help but say "Holy".

Worship is an expression of praise and thanksgiving. The scripture tells us those in heaven give glory, honour, and thanks.

How do you give something to someone who has everything? How do you give the ultimate Giver something in return for all He has done for you?

You give Him your words.

We give him the only thing that we can give him:

Glory
and honour
and thanks.

Glory- "There's no God like you. Nobody can do what you can do, Jesus. All things are possible with you. You split the seas. You move the mountains. You cause the earth to spin, the wind to blow, the waters to rise and cease."

Honour- "Jesus, your name is above all others. You are the author and finisher of my faith. It is by Your name all things are possible. You are King of kings and Lord of lords. There is none higher, there is none better. I praise You because You alone are worthy of my praise."

Thanksgiving- "Thank you, Lord, for saving me. Thank you for saving my family. Thank you for creating me and writing my name in the Book of Life. I am grateful for Your sacrifice. I am grateful for Your love. I am grateful You bore stripes for healing, You took on my sins, You conquered death so I can live with You forever in eternity.

When we start giving glory, and honour, and thanks, those around us can't help but see how good Jesus is. He really can do it all. He really is worthy.

> "Let the words of my mouth, and the meditation of my heart, be acceptable in thy sight, O Lord, my strength, and my redeemer" (Psalms 19:14).

HEALING

"The Lord doth build up Jerusalem: he gathereth together the outcasts of Israel. He healeth the broken in heart, and bindeth up their wounds. He tell the number of the stars; he calleth them all by their names. Great is our Lord, and of great power: his understanding is infinite."

- Psalm 147:3-5

This passage tells us of the Lord building up Jerusalem, but today we can read it for ourselves as God building up His church. We know that church is not just a building, but the church is made of people, specifically, Jesus followers. We are the church.

Right after we read, "The Lord doth build up Jerusalem" we see where, "he gathereth together the outcasts of Israel." Jerusalem is a city in Israel and when the Israelites were captured and taken hostage, they weren't just taken out of Jerusalem, but out of Israel, their country. Whenever they were taken out of where they were supposed to be, God made it His mission to bring them back.

He builds up His church and gathers the outcasts.

You and I may think of ourselves as outcasts. Being human is to be a sinner. Sin makes us want to separate ourselves, but we have been called to unity in Christ, with His church. The Lord is building you up, so He can gather you together and take you back to where you were always meant to be.

How does He build you up so He can bring you back? He healeth the broken in heart, and bindeth up their wounds.

Wounds are the results of what has hurt us. I don't know anybody who escapes this life without some wounds, it just isn't possible. We are born tender hearted, our life is precious, are emotions are real. Wounds will happen and not just wounds, but deep wounds.

We can study the Bible all we want. We can learn every name, every story, every word, but if we do not let God work in us it is all in vain. Knowing is not the same as experiencing. We must experience the healing power of God in our lives through the outpouring of the Holy Ghost. He heals the broken in heart and binds up their wounds.

There are ways that we try to heal our own wounds.

One way is to keep them covered and forget they are there. Have you ever left a band-aid on too long because you didn't want to look at what was underneath? You just try to forget about it and say, "It'll be alright."

Another way is to tell everyone about our wounds. People who care or don't care. We tell anyone and everyone in the hopes that somebody will say or do the right thing.

As long as we keep playing doctor, we will never be healed. It takes a trained physician to fix those deep hurts. A wounded heart left untreated leads to a wounded spirit.

> "But do thou for me, O God the Lord, for thy name's sake: because thy mercy is good, deliver thou me. For I am poor and needy, and my heart is wounded within me" (Psalm 109:21-22).
>
> "The spirit of a man will sustain his infirmity; but a wounded spirit who can bear" (Proverbs 18:14)?

These wounds come from words and actions that hurt us. Maybe they come from sins committed against us or life circumstances that just arose and the product was pain. Other people's "stuff" can cause us pain and our "stuff" can cause other people pain. This is the nature of living. Maybe you have heard the phrase "hurt people hurt people"?

Take for example the man at the tombs who was full of pain:

> And they came over unto the other side of the sea, into the country of the Gadarenes. And when he was come out of the ship, immediately there met him out of the tombs a man with an unclean spirit, Who had his dwelling among the tombs; and no man could bind him, no, not with chains: Because that he had been often bound with fetters and chains, and the chains had been plucked asunder by him, and the fetters broken in pieces: neither could any man tame him. And always, night and day, he was in the mountains, and in the tombs, crying, and cutting himself with stones. But when he saw Jesus afar off, he ran and worshipped him, And cried with a loud

> voice, and said, What have I to do with thee, Jesus, thou Son of the most high God? I adjure thee by God, that thou torment me not. For he said unto him, Come out of the man, thou unclean spirit.
>
> -Mark 5:1-8

This man was seen night and day, cutting himself and crying out. His inner pain manifest through the outer pain of cutting himself. Cutting is a manifestation of the spirit of pain.

We can tell what kind of spirit we are dealing with based on the words used. The man ran and worshipped Jesus, but his words gave him away. He said, "torment me not." We know that Jesus is not the tormentor, so who is doing the speaking? Jesus torments the tormentor. Jesus has authority over the enemy. The spirits that are tormenting you don't want to leave. They are comfortable right where they are, but in the Name of Jesus, I say every torment must flee. Pain must depart in the name of Jesus.

Jesus is our healer.

So how do we mend wounds through the Lord?

Have you ever heard of packing a wound? I looked it up and honestly, it is gross. There were pictures of big, gaping wounds stuffed with gauze then sown together. The reason you pack a wound is so the inside will heal. If the wound is deep and complicated there is a chance that only the covering will heal and the inner tissue will not, so doctors pack it to distribute the healing throughout.

Jesus is that ointment. We pack our wounds so full of Jesus that his healing touch reaches the very depth of the cut. Song of Solomon tells us "Thy name is as ointment poured forth." When we speak the name of Jesus, we are calling forth healing. Everything we do should be done in the name of Jesus. We should move in His name, pray in His name, submit in His name:

> But he was wounded for our transgressions, he was bruised for our iniquities: the chastisement of our peace was upon him; and with his stripes we are healed.
>
> -Isaiah 53:5

ISN'T HE WONDERFUL?

"For unto us a child is born, unto us a son is given: and the government shall be upon his shoulder: and his name shall be called Wonderful, Counsellor, The mighty God, The everlasting Father, The Prince of Peace. Of the increase of his government and peace there shall be no end, upon the throne of David, and upon his kingdom, to order it, and to establish it with judgment and with justice from henceforth even for ever. The zeal of the Lord of hosts will perform this."

- Isaiah 9:6-7

If I was to make a top ten list of verses, Isaiah 9:6 would be on my list. I love the description Isaiah gives of Jesus. He calls Him Wonderful. Councellor. Mighty God. Everlasting Father. Prince of Peace. Just saying those words out loud is enough to get your spirit stirred up.

Do you have this relationship with Jesus?
Can you call Him Wonderful?

Has He been good to you? Has He brought you out of darkness into His marvelous light? Do you stand in awe of who Jesus is? Are you enamored by the fact that He talks to you, that the God of the Universe who set the planets in motion knows your name, and that His thoughts towards you cannot be numbered, "For I know the thoughts that I think toward you, saith the Lord, thoughts of peace, and not of evil, to give you an expected end" (Jeremiah 29:11).

Is He your Councellor?

Do you talk to Him about your problems? Does He guide you into peace? When nobody else in the world, not one single person, can understand how you feel, is He the one you run to?

> "Trust in the Lord with all thine heart; and lean not unto thine own understanding. In all thy ways acknowledge him, and he shall direct thy paths" (Proverbs 3:5-6).

Is He a Mighty God to you?

Do you recognize His authority over your life? Fully God, fully man, who is able to perform miracles and forgive sins. The only One through whom all things are possible. The One who parts the waters for YOU. The One who holds the keys to the kingdom.

> "But Jesus beheld them, and said unto them, With men this is impossible; but with God all things are possible" (Matthew 19:26).

Do you cry out to Him, Everlasting Father? Is He your provider? This is a revelation. Within Jesus are all the riches of glory. It is His heart to see you fulfilled in your life and your calling.

> "Jesus saith unto him, Have I been so long time with you, and yet hast thou not known me, Philip? he that hath seen me hath seen the Father; and how sayest thou then, Show us the Father" (John 14:9)?

Do you recognize Him as your Prince of Peace? The government rests on His shoulders. The same shoulders that carried the cross carry the whole of the universe. Everything rests on who Jesus is, His Word. His ability to perform His plans. It isn't peace as the world gives, but unspeakable joy in knowing there is something after this life. The life you receive because He has overcome death.

> "Be still, and know that I am God: I will be exalted among the heathen, I will be exalted in the earth" (Psalm 46:10).

Do you know who your God is? This God you worship. Are you willing to dedicate your life to learning who Jesus is? Paul talks about Jesus by saying "the unsearchable riches of Christ" (Ephesians 3:8). Who can know all there is to know of God? We could live a thousand years and never come close.

Sometimes we get frustrated. We want to check Jesus off our list. We want to say "I've done that- I've studied. I've read. Give me a certificate. Let me get on my way to something else." But Jesus is saying "I'm a life-long commitment. You'll never get to the bottom of this heart. You'll never get Me figured out. But what you can do, what I offer you, is the opportunity to spend your life learning from Me."

So many times, we just pray for the next miracle we need. Our relationship with Jesus is based on the next need we have. It's "God I'm in need. I'm in need. I'm in need." Boom, He answers our prayer, and we say to ourselves, "Oh, good. I can take a break now. I don't have to pray so hard."

Jesus is wonderful because of who He is. His heart. The way He moves with compassion. He touches the untouchable. He is full of tender mercies and lovingkindness. You are the bride of Jesus, an important part of the great church that He is coming back for.

> "Deep calleth unto deep at the noise of thy waterspouts: all thy waves and thy billows are gone over me. Yet the Lord will command his lovingkindness in the day time, and in the night his song shall be with me, and my prayer unto the God of my life" (Psalm 42:7-8).

THE JOY OF SACRIFICE

"Then the same day at evening, being the first day of the week, when the doors were shut where the disciples were assembled for fear of the Jews, came Jesus and stood in the midst, and saith unto them, Peace be unto you. And when he had so said, he shewed unto them his hands and his side. Then were the disciples glad, when they saw the Lord. Then said Jesus to them again, Peace be unto you: as my Father hath sent me, even so send I you. And when he had said this, he breathed on them, and saith unto them, Receive ye the Holy Ghost: Whose soever sins ye remit, they are remitted unto them; and whose soever sins ye retain, they are retained. But Thomas, one of the twelve, called Didymus, was not with them when Jesus came. The other disciples therefore said unto him, We have seen the Lord. But he said unto them, Except I shall see in his hands the print of the nails, and put my finger into the print of the nails, and thrust my hand into his side, I will not believe. And after eight days again his disciples were within, and Thomas with them: then came Jesus, the doors being shut, and stood in the midst, and said, Peace be unto you. Then saith he to Thomas, Reach hither thy finger, and behold my hands; and reach hither thy hand, and thrust it into my side: and be not faithless, but believing. And Thomas answered and said unto him, My Lord and my God."

-John 20:24-28

After Jesus died, He came back to the disciples, showed them that it was indeed Him, the risen savior, and breathed the Holy Ghost into His friends.

But Thomas wasn't there.

Thomas missed that life-changing moment. We don't know where he was, the scripture doesn't say, but we know he missed it. You and I cannot afford to miss Jesus.

When the disciples later came to Thomas to tell him he had missed the Lord, Thomas was in denial, thinking, "No, not possible, I don't believe it. What you are saying is too spectacular for me to believe. I won't believe it until I see it for myself." Jesus, however, never wants us to dwell in a place of disbelief.

He is always calling us towards faith. He came back and told Thomas, "Here…touch. See for yourself. Here is My hand. Here is My side." I believe Jesus said this not out of a place of condemnation, but excitement and love. Jesus entered with the spirit of, "PEACE. Peace, Thomas. Don't doubt. Peace, Thomas. Don't question what you know to be true. Peace, Thomas. Don't let your pain get in the way of the gospel. Enter my joy. Enter my sacrifice." It was at that very moment when Jesus called Thomas into a greater faith, "Reach higher, put your hand into My side. Get a hold of this sacrifice. See what I overcame. I was dead, but now I am alive."

When it looked like Thomas missed the greatest thing to have ever happened, Jesus said "No, I'm just giving you a chance at greater faith."

Jesus says to us, "I just need you to have more faith. It looks like you missed your chance. It looks like you made the wrong choice at the wrong time, but really, I just need you to believe a little more. I need you to get a hold of this gospel that lives inside of Me. I need you to hold on to Me."

> "And he that searcheth the hearts knoweth what is the mind of the Spirit, because he maketh intercession for the saints according to the will of God. And we know that all things work together for good to them that love God, to them who are the called according to his purpose. For whom he did foreknow, he also did predestinate to be conformed to the image of his Son, that he might be the firstborn among many brethren. Moreover whom he did predestinate, them he also called: and whom he called, them he also justified: and whom he justified, them he also glorified. What shall we then say to these things? If God be for us, who can be against us?" (Romans 8: 27-31).

We are called to be the image of Christ. Our sacrifice draws others around us into greater faith, "The sacrifices of God are a broken spirit: a broken and a contrite heart, O God, thou wilt not despise" (Psalms 51:17).

If your sacrifice doesn't break you, it isn't a sacrifice. If your sacrifice doesn't rid you of your flesh, it isn't a sacrifice. If your sacrifice doesn't cause you to cry out to God, it isn't a sacrifice.

The book of Acts refers to Jesus' death, burial, and resurrection as "His passion." There must be a point where your sacrifice and your passion intersect.

Our redemption was His passion. The cross was His sacrifice. Bartholomew, also known as Nathanael, was a disciple of Jesus. He was commissioned to be a missionary and sent to India. According to history, he was killed by being skinned alive and beheaded. I think the message in Bartholomew's death is that our sacrifice to God, living out his commission, is going to rid us of our flesh.

Men and women of God are imprisoned and tortured all over the world, living out the testimony of Christ in their own bodies, bearing Paul's own statement, "From henceforth let no man trouble me: for I bear in my body the marks of the Lord Jesus" (Galatians 6:17).

Jesus made Himself as nothing. God, robed in flesh, made Himself like us. He served us. Ministered to us. Died for us.

> "But made himself of no reputation, and took upon him the form of a servant, and was made in the likeness of men: And being found in fashion as a man, he humbled himself, and became obedient unto death, even the death of the cross. Wherefore God also hath highly exalted him, and given him a name which is above every name: That at the name of Jesus every knee should bow, of things in heaven, and things in earth, and things under the earth;" (Philippians 2:7-10).

Where in your life can you put your hand in His side? Where can you have more faith? He is inviting you into His sacrifice. Where can you add your passion? This is how you find your joy.

EVERY PLACE

"By faith Abraham, when he was called to go out into a place which he should after receive for an inheritance, obeyed; and he went out, not knowing whither he went."

-Hebrews 11:8

Place means the space you occupy, as in "This is the place I live." It means events that occur, as in "This message will take place." It also means to establish, as in "The President was placed in office."

Place is significant in the Bible, and it is significant in your life. If you are in God's will, then your place has been appointed. Being in the stream of God's will means the Lord moves you from place to place. When Jesus called the disciples, He called them from the place they were to the places they would go. They didn't know what lay ahead, all they knew was that they were following Jesus.

Abraham was called into a place he knew nothing about. All he knew was it was God that called him and if God called him then he would be obedient, trusting that God is good and whatever He had for Abraham was good. Trusting God and moving in that trust is faith. His sons had the same promise as Abraham. The promise went from generation to generation.

Scripture tells us that as Abraham went, he looked for a city with foundations, because he knew God only builds with a strong foundation. The devil is interested in collapsing something, but God is in the business of building something. And if God builds it, then it must be strong.

When you are built by God, you become the place.

Here is the story of Jacob's (Abraham's son) place:
> And Jacob went out from Beersheba, and went toward Haran. And he lighted upon a certain place, and tarried there all night, because the sun was set; and he took of the stones of that place, and put them for his pillows, and lay down in that place to sleep. And he dreamed, and behold a ladder set up on the earth, and the top of it reached to heaven: and behold the angels of God ascending and descending on it. And, behold, the Lord stood above it, and said, I am the Lord God of Abraham thy father, and the God of Isaac: the land whereon thou liest, to thee will I give it, and to thy seed; And thy seed shall be as the dust of the earth, and thou shalt spread abroad to the west, and to the east, and to the north, and to the south: and in thee and in thy seed shall all the families of the earth be blessed. And, behold, I am with thee, and will keep thee in all places whither thou goest, and will bring thee again into this land; for I will not leave thee, until I have done that which I have spoken to thee of. And Jacob awaked out of his sleep, and he said, Surely the Lord is in this place; and I

knew it not. And he was afraid, and said, How dreadful is this place! this is none other but the house of God, and this is the gate of heaven. And Jacob rose up early in the morning, and took the stone that he had put for his pillows, and set it up for a pillar, and poured oil upon the top of it. And he called the name of that place Bethel: but the name of that city was called Luz at the first. And Jacob vowed a vow, saying, If God will be with me, and will keep me in this way that I go, and will give me bread to eat, and raiment to put on, So that I come again to my father's house in peace; then shall the Lord be my God: And this stone, which I have set for a pillar, shall be God's house: and of all that thou shalt give me I will surely give the tenth unto thee.

-Genesis 28:10-22

Jacob was established in Bethel. He encountered God in Bethel. It was in this place that God said "I will keep thee in all places…" What God does for you in one place, He will carry over into the next place. If He blesses you here, He will bless you there. If He makes you strong here, you will be strong there. Don't be scared to leave a place. It is not the place that makes you who you are, it is the foundations that have been built. Your builder and maker is God, and He goes with you to every place:

> And it shall come to pass, if thou shalt hearken diligently unto the voice of the Lord

thy God, to observe and to do all his commandments which I command thee this day, that the Lord thy God will set thee on high above all nations of the earth: And all these blessings shall come on thee, and overtake thee, if thou shalt hearken unto the voice of the Lord thy God. Blessed shalt thou be in the city, and blessed shalt thou be in the field. Blessed shall be the fruit of thy body, and the fruit of thy ground, and the fruit of thy cattle, the increase of thy kine, and the flocks of thy sheep. Blessed shall be thy basket and thy store. Blessed shalt thou be when thou comest in, and blessed shalt thou be when thou goest out.

- Deuteronomy 28: 1-6

You are the "thy" and the "thou" in the blessing. It isn't the place that blesses you, it is your obedience and commitment to the Lord that causes you to be blessed:

> Let not your heart be troubled: ye believe in God, believe also in me. In my Father's house are many mansions: if it were not so, I would have told you. I go to prepare a place for you. And if I go and prepare a place for you, I will come again, and receive you unto myself; that where I am, there ye may be also. And whither I go ye know, and the way ye know.
>
> -John 14:1-4

Jesus said, "Where I am, there ye may also be." That place is prepared. You are prepared. Jesus wants you to be prepared for what He has for you. He will be with you in the way that you go because He is the way that you go.

You and I are grafted into Abraham and Jacob's promise. Jacob would later be renamed Israel (a place, a people). You and I inherit the promises of Israel through the sacrifice of Jesus. To be grafted in means we are tied to the original root system. If it were not for Jesus, you and I would have no hope of making it to heaven. We would be gentiles, cursed because of our own genetics. Our heritage and the people we come from would have been a curse to us.

To graft a plant means you take a shoot from one plant and bind it to a stronger plant. The strength of the rooted plant sustains the shoot until the two grow together as one.

Some reasons why plants are grafted in:
Take advantage of strong roots- to be strong in Jesus.
Repair damaged plants- to be overcomers in all things.
Increase growth- to grow in knowledge of Christ.
Optimize pollination- for us this means spreading the Gospel.

One of our greatest blessings is the heart of God and His desire that none are lost. Because He is rich in mercy, He found a way that you and I could be a part of the bloodline. Because of Jesus' work on the cross, the blood shed for us, and the infilling of His Spirit, we are grafted into the promises of Abraham, and Isaac, and Jacob. That God of the Old Testament is the God of the New Testament. He raised up a man named Paul to go and seek out gentiles so that we too may be blessed. We are partakers of the original promise of Abraham. The promise that says I will be with you wherever you go. I am with you here and I will be with you there. I will be with you in all places and in all things:

> To every thing there is a season, and a time to every purpose under the heaven: A time to be born, and a time to die; a time to plant, and a time to pluck up that which is planted;
>
> - Ecclesiastes 3:1-2

If you are in the season of being planted, stay and let the Lord build strong foundations. If you are in the season of being plucked up, get excited, and receive His promise to be with you always in all things in all places.

STAR CHASERS

"And God said, Let there be lights in the firmament of the heaven to divide the day from the night; and let them be for signs, and for seasons, and for days, and years: And let them be for lights in the firmament of the heaven to give light upon the earth: and it was so. And God made two great lights; the greater light to rule the day, and the lesser light to rule the night: he made the stars also. And God set them in the firmament of the heaven to give light upon the earth, And to rule over the day and over the night, and to divide the light from the darkness: and God saw that it was good."
- Genesis 1:14-18

At the beginning of the world, God created. He created light to divide the darkness. The sun and the moon and the stars. They would be for signs, seasons, and to show the passing of time. God would use these natural things to prove to us the supernatural.

A sign is a signal of something greater. It is the gust of wind that blows before the storm or the flower that blooms before Spring.

Signs prove to us that something invisible is taking place, but Jesus warned us that our faith should not be based on signs:
> The Pharisees also with the Sadducees came, and tempting desired him that he would shew them a sign from heaven. He answered and said unto them, When it is evening, ye say, It will be fair weather: for the sky is red. And in the morning, It

will be foul weather to day: for the sky is red and lowering. O ye hypocrites, ye can discern the face of the sky; but can ye not discern the signs of the times? A wicked and adulterous generation seeketh after a sign; and there shall no sign be given unto it, but the sign of the prophet Jonas. And he left them, and departed.

- Matthew 16:1-4

Asking Jesus for a sign is a dangerous habit. When we ask for a sign, what we are saying is "I don't believe You are who You say You are. Prove Yourself to me." God does not have to prove Himself to us. Because He is kind and generous, He shares Himself with us and demonstrates His love towards us. Asking for a sign is an act of pride and proves to Him our lack of faith.

As His followers, His signs follow us. When people see us move in the Lord, they take our work as the invisible God being made visible through faith. In the book of Matthew, we learn how God uses the stars to lead a group of worshipers called wise men to the miracle of His birth here on earth:

> Now when Jesus was born in Bethlehem of Judaea in the days of Herod the king, behold, there came wise men from the east to Jerusalem, Saying, Where is he that is born King of the Jews? for we have seen his star in the east, and are come to worship him. When Herod the king had heard these things, he was troubled, and all Jerusalem with him. And

> when he had gathered all the chief priests and scribes of the people together, he demanded of them where Christ should be born. And they said unto him, In Bethlehem of Judaea: for thus it is written by the prophet, And thou Bethlehem, in the land of Juda, art not the least among the princes of Juda: for out of thee shall come a Governor, that shall rule my people Israel. Then Herod, when he had privily called the wise men, enquired of them diligently what time the star appeared. And he sent them to Bethlehem, and said, Go and search diligently for the young child; and when ye have found him, bring me word again, that I may come and worship him also.
> - Matthew 2: 1-8

The wise men saw a star and began to follow.

We follow things all the time.

We follow people's lives. What they are up to. How things are going for them. We follow social media accounts. The latest headlines. Covid numbers. There is a lot in the world asking us to follow, but Jesus said to follow Him. Follow Him into healing. Follow Him into sobriety. Follow Him into righteousness. Follow Him into purpose:

> And Jesus, walking by the sea of Galilee, saw two brethren, Simon called Peter, and Andrew his brother, casting a net into the sea: for they were fishers. And he saith unto them, Follow

me, and I will make you fishers of men. And they straightway left their nets, and followed him.

- Matthew 4: 18-20

The wise men left everything and went on the hunt for this child. They had so much faith that they thought it possible their future could rest on the shoulders of a baby. They went straight to Jerusalem and asked to see the King of the Jews. They saw a sign and looked for Jesus. By doing so, they created a stir in the atmosphere. Everyone started talking and asking, "Who is this King of the Jews?"

Herod got worried. The Word says he met with them privately. When you start chasing after Jesus, you find yourself in interesting situations. The wise men just wanted to worship, but Herod wanted them to help him in committing a sin.

We must be wise as serpents and harmless as doves (Matthew 10:16). We must try the spirits and know who and what we are dealing with (1 John 4:1-5). Herod was taken over by a spirit of murder and jealousy. The enemy was trying to create a trap:

> When they had heard the king, they departed; and, lo, the star, which they saw in the east, went before them, till it came and stood over where the young child was. When they saw the star, they rejoiced with exceeding great joy. And when they were come into the house, they saw the young child with Mary his

> mother, and fell down, and worshipped him: and when they had opened their treasures, they presented unto him gifts; gold, and frankincense and myrrh.
>
> - Matthew 2: 9-11

Notice their reaction…

They found Jesus and rejoiced. What must it have been like to be there? The atmosphere. The angels. God in flesh. The One who created the star they followed was there in front of them. The one who created the world with His words, was lying there unable to speak.

If we ever feel that we are in charge, God has a few questions for us:

> Where wast thou when I laid the foundations of the earth? declare, if thou hast understanding. Who hath laid the measures thereof, if thou knowest? or who hath stretched the line upon it? Whereupon are the foundations thereof fastened? or who laid the corner stone thereof; When the morning stars sang together, and all the sons of God shouted for joy? Or who shut up the sea with doors, when it brake forth, as if it had issued out of the womb? When I made the cloud the garment thereof, and thick darkness a swaddlingband for it, And brake up for it my decreed place, and set bars and doors, And said, Hitherto shalt thou come, but no further:

> and here shall thy proud waves be stayed? Hast thou commanded the morning since thy days; and caused the dayspring to know his place; That it might take hold of the ends of the earth, that the wicked might be shaken out of it?
>
> - Job 38: 4-13

What was the rightful way for the wise men to respond to this God, this child who carried the weight of glory in His tiny body? Worship. Worship is an act of adoration. With our worship we say, "All of me, for all of You. Here, Jesus. Take everything I have. Here, Jesus. You deserve glory. You deserve honor. You deserve it all. All of me, for all of You."

The wise men fell at His feet and worshipped. It was only after worship that they began to open their treasures. It was only after they acknowledged His holiness that what they brought with them was worth anything:

> And they that be wise shall shine as the brightness of the firmament; and they that turn many to righteousness as the stars for ever and ever.
>
> - Daniel 12:3

God doesn't want your gifts first, He wants your worship first. Learn how to worship and your gifts will present themselves. Learn how to sit at His feet and your gifts will become valuable.

THE PRAYER WHEEL

"Be careful for nothing; but in every thing by prayer and supplication with thanksgiving let your requests be made known unto God."

-Philippians 4:6

Prayer is communication between you and Jesus. In order to successfully communicate there is a giving and receiving of information. One sided conversations aren't very much fun. If we just talk to Jesus, we will soon get weary of the talking. It is the back and forth of knowledge and ideas that builds a relationship. Jesus is in the business of relationship. He doesn't want just a casual relationship; He wants one that will stand the test of time. The kind where you grow and mature in Him and are enriched by your time together. He longs to hear your voice and see your face. When you don't seek Him out, He misses you.

The Israelites wondered away from the heart of the Lord because they didn't spend the time and effort it took to know Him personally. We serve a God who wants to be the biggest part of our life.

Sometimes we pray together in unity, but I think most often our prayer is just one-on-one. We make time for Him. Jesus becomes so much a part of us that it is natural for us to talk to Him. How amazing is it that God built within us a way to communicate with Him: our thoughts, our words, the meditations of our heart? We are vessels designed to give and receive His Words. 1 Thessalonians 5:17 tells us to "pray without ceasing." This means we never stop praying. We live and move and have our being in this constant spirit of conversation with the Lord.

The environment God has placed us in and the people He has surrounded us with are the food for our prayer life. We are continually checking what we see against the Word of God and translating that awareness into a prayer.

Translate is also to transfer, to move places:
> By faith Enoch was translated that he should not see death; and was not found, because God had translated him: for before his translation he had this testimony, that he pleased God. Enoch was translated from an earthly realm to a heavenly realm. We take what we see on earth and we translate it into a heavenly realm using our voice, our heart, the Word of God, and His Spirit.
> - Hebrews 11:5

Prayer is a process that happens within us.

I work at a rice mill with my family. The rice is sown into the grown, harvested after it grows, and is taken to the mill. At the mill it starts as something you cannot eat. The hull on the outside must first be taken off. The rice goes through a milling process to get something people can put on their plate and feed to their family. There is a process that must first take place.

Prayer is the milling process for us. We see something or hear something or need something that awakens our Spirit, it is beyond us. It is something only Jesus can handle, so we take it to the mill of prayer.

In the old days, milling was done with two big stones. They were round and flat. One stone would sit on top of the other. The bottom stone didn't move, but the top stone was turned in a circular motion. Prayer is like this milling process. Jesus is that bottom stone. He doesn't move. His Word doesn't change. His character never falters. He is our stability.

We are the top stone. We are driven to prayer. We move according to His Word. We influence His Will with our supplications. Our voice gives the prayer momentum. Our heart sets out on a journey to reach His heart. He welcomes us into His chambers. We go boldly before the throne. The outcome of the conversation is the product of two forces coming together. Our needs and His ability. It is a collision.

> "And from the days of John the Baptist until now the kingdom of heaven suffereth violence, and the violent take it by force" (Matthew 11:12).

There should be a force to your prayer life. You have to come against the devil's agenda and take back the will of God for your life, your family, your country, this world. God has a specific will, a way He wants things to go, you and I must pray that will.

> "Verily I say unto you, Whatsoever ye shall bind on earth shall be bound in heaven: and whatsoever ye shall loose on earth shall be loosed in heaven" (Matthew 18:18).

We bind our mind and our testimonies to the mind and testimony of Jesus. We bind the lies and tactics of the enemy and send them back to the pit of hell. We bind the strongman that comes against our house. We lose God's will and purpose for our lives. We lose blessings over those we love. We lose the grip of strongholds from the serpent who comes against God's people. We do all this through our words. The words of our mouth, the outpourings of our heart, the groanings of the Spirit.

> "Death and life are in the power of the tongue: and they that love it shall eat the fruit thereof" (Proverbs 18:21).
>
> "Likewise the Spirit also helpeth our infirmities: for we know not what we should pray for as we ought: but the Spirit itself maketh intercession for us with groanings which cannot be uttered" (Romans 8:26).

Ezekiel tells us of a vision the prophet had in captivity. Heaven was opened to him, and he saw four creatures. They had the body of humans, but four faces. The face of a man, a lion, an ox, and an eagle. This is a very complex vision, and I won't pretend to be smart enough to interpret it completely, but I did notice in part that these creatures were bound to the Spirit of God.

This is the Message version of Ezekiel:

> As I watched the four creatures, I saw something that looked like a wheel on the ground beside each of the four-faced creatures. This is what the wheels looked like: They were identical wheels, sparkling like diamonds in the sun. It looked like they were wheels within wheels, like a gyroscope. They went in any one of the four directions they faced, but straight, not veering off. The rims were immense, circled with eyes. When the living creatures went, the wheels went; when the living creatures lifted off, the wheels lifted off. Wherever the spirit went, they went, the wheels sticking right with them, for the spirit of the living creatures was in the wheels. When the creatures went, the wheels went; when the creatures stopped, the wheels stopped; when the creatures lifted off, the wheels lifted off, because the spirit of the living creatures was in the wheels.
>
> -Ezekiel 1:15-21

It was the Spirit of God, the creatures, and the wheels. They stuck together and moved as one. This is how we should be. Us moving in the Spirit, the Spirit moving through us, and the wheel of prayer right next to us. What I am trying to get across is that prayer should be so much a part of who we are that it is inseparable from who we are. To pray without ceasing means we never stop. The same way you cannot detach yourself from your right hand, but your right hand is always with you, you are always using it as you go throughout your day. Prayer is a tool God has given you to achieve His purpose. Not only to achieve His purpose, but it is also your purpose. You are to be moved to prayer and move through prayer. A wheel within a wheel.

Our prayers are wheels within wheels. One prayer leads to another prayer which leads to another. We are driven from glory to glory and from faith to faith by our love for Jesus and our desire to speak to Him and know what is on the Master's heart.

> "But seek ye first the kingdom of God, and his righteousness; and all these things shall be added unto you" (Matthew 6:33).

THE FATHER OF LIGHTS

"Every good gift and every perfect gift are from above, and cometh down from the Father of lights, with whom is no variableness, neither shadow of turning."

- James 1:17

This passage in James describes Jesus as the "Father of Lights." A beautiful title. In Genesis, one of God's first acts was to create light:

> God said, Let there be light and there was light. And God saw the light, that it was good: and God divided the light from the darkness. And God called the light Day, and the darkness he called Night. And the evening and the morning were the first day.
>
> -Genesis 1:3-5

He created light and then separated it from darkness. There has always been a difference between light and dark. 1 John 1:5 says, "This then is the message which we have heard of him, and declare unto you, that God is light, and in him is no darkness at all." You and I, as Jesus followers, cannot live in twilight or dusk, we cannot be a little light and a little dark. In God there is no darkness. He is the Father of lights; therefore, you and I must only be light. Our life's objective is to drive out the darkness wherever it hides. The darkness in our own life and the darkness that exists in the world. Our sphere of influence must be so bright that when others enter, they too are awakened. It's hard to sleep with the lights on. Sometimes our call is to just be the lightbulb in the room, but there are times, special moments, that you are going to shine so bright because the glory of God will rest on you.

Moses was a friend to God. Moses was under submission to the Lord, but he also communed with Him. They talked together. Spent time together. They had a relationship. There was a back and forth to their words. God would speak, then Moses would reply. Moses would speak, then God would answer. They shared ideas with one another. God could trust Moses with who He was. He revealed Himself to Moses.

When you have a relationship like that with Jesus it will be evident. Personal time with the Lord changes you in ways you cannot predict, and you cannot control:

> And the Lord said unto Moses, Write thou these words: for after the tenor of these words I have made a covenant with thee and with Israel. And he was there with the Lord forty days and forty nights; he did neither eat bread, nor drink water. And he wrote upon the tables the words of the covenant, the ten commandments. And it came to pass, when Moses came down from mount Sinai with the two tables of testimony in Moses' hand, when he came down from the mount, that Moses wist not that the skin of his face shone while he talked with him. And when Aaron and all the children of Israel saw Moses, behold, the skin of his face shone; and they were afraid to come nigh him. And Moses called unto them; and Aaron and all the rulers of the congregation returned unto him: and Moses talked with them. And afterward

> all the children of Israel came nigh: and he gave them in commandment all that the Lord had spoken with him in mount Sinai. And till Moses had done speaking with them, he put a vail on his face. But when Moses went in before the Lord to speak with him, he took the vail off, until he came out. And he came out, and spake unto the children of Israel that which he was commanded. And the children of Israel saw the face of Moses, that the skin of Moses' face shone: and Moses put the vail upon his face again, until he went in to speak with him.
>
> - Exodus 34:27-35

When Moses came off that mountain, he didn't know that his face was glowing with the glory of God, all he knew was he had spent time with the Lord. Moses was a literal, shining beacon of light to those around him.

The reason the day is bright is because of the sun. There is a source to our brightness. We in ourselves are naturally dark, but Jesus became the Son so we could partake in His light and shine. He will take what worked against us and redeem it for His glory. Moses was a murderer and yet God used Him to free millions. We must choose, will we be darkness, or will we be light? We cannot be both. Read the Word of the Lord for you:

> For brass I will bring gold, and for iron I will bring silver, and for wood brass, and for stones iron: I will also make thy officers peace, and thine exactors righteousness. Violence shall no more be heard in thy

land, wasting nor destruction within thy borders; but thou shalt call thy walls Salvation, and thy gates Praise. The sun shall be no more thy light by day; neither for brightness shall the moon give light unto thee: but the Lord shall be unto thee an everlasting light, and thy God thy glory. Thy sun shall no more go down; neither shall thy moon withdraw itself: for the Lord shall be thine everlasting light, and the days of thy mourning shall be ended. Thy people also shall be all righteous: they shall inherit the land for ever, the branch of my planting, the work of my hands, that I may be glorified. A little one shall become a thousand, and a small one a strong nation: I the Lord will hasten it in his time.

- Isaiah 60:17-22

Your walls are called Salvation.
Your gates are called Praise.
Your sun is Jesus.
Your hope is Glory.

We are the work of His hands. The result of His planting. In this world there is light and there is dark, but in heaven there is only Jesus. We must choose now, this day, who we will serve (Joshua 24:15). Jesus gives us a parable of light and dark. In His right hand are those who do His will and in His left are those who do nothing. Nothing is as consequential as evil. Doing nothing is a choice:

> Then shall the King say unto them on his right hand, Come, ye blessed of my Father, inherit the kingdom prepared for you from the foundation of the world: For I was an

> hungred, and ye gave me meat: I was thirsty, and ye gave me drink: I was a stranger, and ye took me in: Naked, and ye clothed me: I was sick, and ye visited me: I was in prison, and ye came unto me. Then shall the righteous answer him, saying, Lord, when saw we thee an hungred, and fed thee? or thirsty, and gave thee drink? When saw we thee a stranger, and took thee in? or naked, and clothed thee? Or when saw we thee sick, or in prison, and came unto thee? And the King shall answer and say unto them, Verily I say unto you, Inasmuch as ye have done it unto one of the least of these my brethren, ye have done it unto me.
>
> - Matthew 25:34-40

The right hand of God is a wonderful place to be. The right hand is for those who show compassion on the least of these, those who help bring heaven to earth. See, in heaven there is no pain, no suffering, no crying, and no sickness. Our job is to bring resolution to other's pain, so it feels like heaven on earth. It feels like Jesus is with them, because He is at work through us.

The left hand is the opposite. The right hand is light, but the left hand is dark. The left hand ignores the needy and does nothing to help the hungry or the naked. The left hand ignores the kingdom of God. They are so preoccupied with the things of the world that they do not see those in need, and if they see them, they certainly don't do anything about it. They are as far from Jesus as you can get:

> Then shall he say also unto them on the left hand, Depart from me, ye cursed, into everlasting fire, prepared for the devil and his angels: For I was an hungred, and ye gave me no meat: I was thirsty, and ye gave me no drink: I was a stranger, and ye took me not in: naked, and ye clothed me not: sick, and in prison, and ye visited me not. Then shall they also answer him, saying, Lord, when saw we thee an hungred, or athirst, or a stranger, or naked, or sick, or in prison, and did not minister unto thee? Then shall he answer them, saying, Verily I say unto you, Inasmuch as ye did it not to one of the least of these, ye did it not to me. And these shall go away into everlasting punishment: but the righteous into life eternal.
>
> - Matthew 25:41-46

Here's the revelation that the right hand gets, but the left hand doesn't understand: Jesus counts His brothers the same as Himself. He is so humble, that when someone does something for us, He says in the kingdom of God that is the same as doing it for Him. This blows my mind to think about. Jesus, fully God and fully man, is so invested in us that when someone blesses us, it blesses Him. He counts it the exact same. He made Himself to be like us in every way possible, He is so entwined with our wellbeing, that when we minister or give to another it's as though we are doing it directly to Jesus. That is a love that is beyond human understanding. There is so much light in Him that our natural eyes cannot perceive it and our mind cannot reason it out. It is out of our love for Him that we naturally do our good works just like it was Moses' friendship that resulted in the glory shining on His face. You don't spend forty days and forty nights with someone you don't really love. You don't write down every word of someone you sort of like. Moses had a love for God that caused Him to be fully devoted. Jesus has a love for us that does the same.

His righteousness causes us to be righteous. If you are wondering, "How do I get to be that good? How do I make sure I'm on the right side of things? How do I know that I am in the right hand and not the left?" The answer will always be "Are you the light or are you the darkness?" From where do you draw your strength? Light begets light, darkness begets darkness.

> "Let your light so shine before men, that they may see your good works, and glorify your Father which is in heaven" (Matthew 5:16).
>
> "Commit thy way unto the Lord; trust also in him; and he shall bring it to pass. And he shall bring forth thy righteousness as the light, and thy judgment as the noonday" (Psalm 37:5-6).

We are going to commit ourselves to only serving the Light that is Jesus Christ. We dwell in light, absorb it within ourselves (our hearts, our minds, our souls, our strength) and we take it will us when we come down from that mountain top where we have spent time with Jesus.

THE END OF A THING

"And I saw in the right hand of him that sat on the throne a book written within and on the backside, sealed with seven seals. And I saw a strong angel proclaiming with a loud voice, Who is worthy to open the book, and to loose the seals thereof? And no man in heaven, nor in earth, neither under the earth, was able to open the book, neither to look thereon. And I wept much, because no man was found worthy to open and to read the book, neither to look thereon. And one of the elders saith unto me, Weep not: behold, the Lion of the tribe of Judah, the Root of David, hath prevailed to open the book, and to loose the seven seals thereof."

- Revelation 5: 1-5

In the beginning of Chapter 5, we see John presented with a question "Who is worthy to open the book, and to loose the seals thereof?" The whole earth was searched and not one person was found to have the ability to do it. Not one in heaven or on earth, billions of people and angelic hosts and nobody was able. John began to weep. It seemed like a lost cause. He was frustrated because here was something that needed to be done and there was nobody able to do the job. Have you ever been in that situation? Have you ever been in a bind, but you weren't able to figure out the solution? Did it bring you to tears like it did John?

Opening the book seemed like a lost cause, but then suddenly someone said "Jesus can do it." Not only could He open the book, but He could loose the seals. He was able to do what He has always done, show up just in time and do the the thing (heal the disease, rebuke the spirit, solve the problem) that nobody else could do. We call this a miracle.

Miracles are supernatural events that have no human explanation. The only way they are possible is through divine intervention. The invisible made visible in and through the lives of men and women. The ultimate source of a miracle is always Jesus, His Spirit working on earth.

There are nine gifts of the Spirit, one of which is the working of miracles. This means that when we are full of the Holy Ghost, walking in the Spirit, you and I have a pretty good shot at operating in this gift. Not only that, but if we pray for the gift of miracles and believe that we will receive it, the Word tells us we can have it:

> For verily I say unto you, That whosoever shall say unto this mountain, Be thou removed, and be thou cast into the sea; and shall not doubt in his heart, but shall believe that those things which he saith shall come to pass; he shall have whatsoever he saith. Therefore I say unto you, What things soever ye desire, when ye pray, believe that ye receive them, and ye shall have them.
> - Mark 11:23-24

To believe means we put credit in the authority of Jesus. When we believe, we know in our hearts that Jesus really is able. We have confidence in Him. We believe on Him. Romans 3:4 says, "Let God be true and every man a liar." Jesus might say, "if you only believe that I am able to do the miraculous in your life, then I'll do it." Faith allows us the opportunity to partake in kingdom work. It takes a miracle to move the mountain, it takes faith to believe it can be moved.

Why would we want the gift of miracles? So, we can have all the stuff and do all the things? Not in God's Kingdom, "Ye ask, and receive not, because ye ask amiss, that ye may consume it upon your lusts" (James 4:3).

That's a pretty harsh rebuke. It causes us to question our motives. Why do we ask for the things we ask for? What is the root of our prayer?

If it is anything beyond "seek ye first the kingdom of God, and His righteousness" then we ask amiss and need to reevaluate why we are asking (Matthew 6:33). There has to be some inner drive that causes us to deny ourselves and seek God's will, no matter the cost. It's the same drive that kept Jesus from calling the angels when He could have been saved. It kept him on the path to Calvary, when He simply could have stopped.

We have examples in the faith to look up to:
> Women received their dead raised to life again: and others were tortured, not accepting deliverance; that they might obtain a better resurrection.
> -Hebrews 11:35

This verse tells us that some experienced the miracle of seeing the dead raised to life, but others, others were tortured and refused deliverance. Think about that, they were so dedicated to the kingdom they denied themselves to receive the ultimate reward, an eternity with Jesus. Man offered them a way out, but they stayed in agony to gain eternity.

The Enemy is trying to extinguish faith from the planet, but you are the keeper of the faith. You were born in a country where you can express that faith in whatever way you choose. You are free to put your faith in action.

What does that look like in your life? Is it stopping to pray for someone you don't know? Giving your testimony to a hurting friend? Feeding the homeless? Writing letters to prisoners? How do you practice your faith in Jesus? How do you exemplify the truth that God wrapped himself in flesh, bore our sins, died on the cross, overcame death, and will return to judge the quick and the dead?

What does that look like in your life, right here, right now? In the very place God has positioned you. How are you preparing to grow stronger in the Lord so you can be an even better witness? We have a responsibility to the One who saved us.

We pray for the gifts of the Spirit, the working of miracles, so we can help advance the Kingdom of God. Others need healing in their bodies, deliverance from their past, and mercy for their loved ones. They need a move of God and God needs willing vessels to work through. You can be that vessel. You can be the one God uses to change a life.

But you can also be the one to receive the miracle. Is it possible the working of miracles refers to how God plans on moving in your life? That miracles are built into your testimony. After all, is it not already a miracle that Jesus lives in you? That you were pulled out of darkness into marvelous light? Your life is not ordinary, but extraordinary.

You are simply waiting for the next miracle to occur:

> Now Peter and John went up together into the temple at the hour of prayer, being the ninth hour. And a certain man lame from his mother's womb was carried, whom they laid daily at the gate of the temple which is called Beautiful, to ask alms of them that entered into the temple; Who seeing Peter and John about to go into the temple asked an alms. And Peter, fastening his eyes upon him with John, said, Look on us. And he gave heed unto them, expecting to receive something of them. Then Peter said, Silver and gold have I none; but such as I have give I thee: In the name of Jesus Christ of Nazareth rise up and walk. And he took him by the right hand, and lifted him up: and immediately his feet and ankle bones received strength. And he leaping up stood, and walked, and entered with them into the temple, walking, and leaping, and praising God. And all the people saw him walking and praising God: And they knew that it was he which sat for alms at the Beautiful gate of the temple: and they were

filled with wonder and amazement at that which had happened unto him. And as the lame man which was healed held Peter and John, all the people ran together unto them in the porch that is called Solomon's, greatly wondering.

-Acts 3: 1-11

This man sat by that gate day after day, asking for money when what he needed was a miracle. He was expecting gold and silver, but what Peter and John had to give him was so much better. Peter and John believed on Jesus, their belief activated the Name, and the Name brought forth a miracle. In the name of Jesus Christ of Nazareth rise up and walk. Some of you are sitting at a gate called Beautiful. You think your time has passed you by. You think "I've been sitting here too long."

There is no timeframe on the miraculous. If we learn anything from the Bible, it is that God likes to move after it seems the time has passed for it to be possible. After Sarah and Abraham passed childbearing years. After Hannah couldn't conceive. After Zechariah and Elizabeth had been childless for so long.

After the whole world is searched for somebody to open the book and lose the seals, *THEN* Jesus shows up.

Scripture tells us, "Better is the end of a thing than the beginning thereof: and the patient in spirit is better than the proud in spirit" (Ecclesiastes 7:8). Believe on God. If it feels like you have been sitting on a shelf, life has passed you by, your best years are behind you, *THEN* you are ripe for the miracle.

> "He that hath an ear, let him hear what the Spirit saith unto the churches. And unto the angel of the church of the Laodiceans write; These things saith the Amen, the faithful and true witness, the beginning of the creation of God;" (Revelation 3:13-14).

Jesus is the Amen. So be it.

CONCLUSION

Our mission in this walk with Jesus is to be victorious. As we walk to the foot of the cross to cover ourselves in the precious blood of Christ, Jesus is walking alongside us, encouraging us to keep fighting the good fight of faith.

While you are hurting, Jesus says "victorious."
While you are broken, Jesus says "victorious."
While you are repenting, Jesus says "victorious."
While you are growing, Jesus says "victorious."

All the while you are overcoming, the Spirit is confirming the truth, the reality of God's presence in your life that you are victorious and more than a conqueror.

Before Jesus was crucified, He prayed for us:

> And now come I to thee; and these things I speak in the world, that they might have my joy fulfilled in themselves. I have given them thy word; and the world hath hated them, because they are not of the world, even as I am not of the world. I pray not that thou shouldest take them out of the world, but that thou shouldest keep them from the evil. They are not of the world, even as I am not of the world. Sanctify them through thy truth: thy word is

> truth. As thou hast sent me into the world, even so have I also sent them into the world. And for their sakes I sanctify myself, that they also might be sanctified through the truth.
>
> -John 17:13-19

According to Jesus' very words, that He spoke so we would have joy, our victory comes from:

Separating yourself from the world.
Sanctifying yourself through His word.
Coming into agreement with His plan.

To paraphrase, Jesus said, "Don't take them out of the world, just keep them from evil." You are to be in the world and not of the world. Sanctify and separate yourself through the Word of God.

Paul said, "But put ye on the Lord Jesus Christ, and make not provision for the flesh, to fulfil the lusts thereof" (Romans 13:14). If you spend enough time in His Word, you will begin to see things through His eyes. You will hear His voice running through your thoughts. Scripture will come to mind in the simplest of moments. The big things of life won't feel so heavy because you will feel the Lord carrying your troubles in the inkwell of scripture. The Word is a river we sit next to, drink from and swim in. His Word will build you into the person you were always meant to become.

Victory Mission Bible Training Center is a division of Mission Teens, Inc., an 8–10-month Christian discipleship program for people with drug, alcohol and/or emotional problems who are willing to seek God as the answer to their problems.

Victory Mission Bible Training Center
Jennifer Jones, Program Director
750 Austin Road
Center Ridge, Arkansas 72027
Phone: 501.386.1493
www.missionteens.com

ABOUT THE AUTHOR

Ashley Ennis is a licensed minister through the Associated Brotherhood of Christians and editor of their publication *Our Herald*. She preaches at Victory Mission Bible Training Center in Center Ridge, Arkansas, a residential program for those overcoming life controlling habits through the Word of God. She is also the Women's Minister and Social Media Director at her church, Plainview Jesus Name Church.

Ashley is blessed to work with her family on their farm, Ralston Family Farms. One of her biggest joys is the opportunity to help in their "Family to Family" rice donation program.

Website: www.ashleyennis.com